SILENCE, D DENIAL

DATE DUE

BEYOND

SILENCE AND DENIAL:

DEATH AND DYING

RECONSIDERED

LUCY BREGMAN

Westminster John Knox Press
Louisville, Kentucky

Scripture quotations marked NIV are from
The Holy Bible, New International Version.
Copyright © 1973, 1978, 1984 International Bible Society.
Used by permission of Zondervan Publishers.

Book design by Sharon Adams
Cover design by PAZ Design Group
Cover photo © 1999 PhotoDisc Inc.

First Edition
Published by Westminster John Knox Press
Louisville, Kentucky

This book is printed on acid-free paper that meets the
American National Standards Institute Z39.48 standard. ∞

PRINTED IN THE UNITED STATES OF AMERICA
99 00 01 02 03 04 05 06 07 08 — 10 9 8 7 6 5 4 3 2

Library of Congress Cataloging-in-Publication Data

Bregman, Lucy.
    Beyond silence and denial : death and dying reconsidered / by Lucy
Bregman. — 1st ed.
        p.   cm.
    Includes bibliographical references and index.
    ISBN 0-664-25802-6 (alk. paper)
    1. Death—Religious aspects—Christianity.   I. Title.
BT825.B72   1999
236′.1—dc21   98-47299

CONTENTS

My thanks to the following persons for their help, insight, and willingness to share their experiences with me: Ms. Carrie Collins, Fr. Michael Tuck, Dr. Sara Thiermann, Prof. Hendrika Vande Kemp, and Prof. Gisela Webb. Also my students, particularly Ms. Helen Black, Ms. Judy Buck-Glenn, Mr. Dugan McGinley, and Ms. Jane McCardell. Finally, my sister Emily Rizzo, for her friendship and support.

Introduction

New Words for Death and Dying

N othing I heard in church helped," the elderly widow stated. "It was only when the psychologist told me, 'Death is a natural event, you must accept it,' that I began to recover from my husband's death." A seminary student echoed this theme. "Once you've said that death is natural, what more is there to say?" he asked rhetorically. These two voices are among many who use a new language for death and dying and grief, a language that is reshaping the way not only our society, but Christians within it think and speak on these topics. The thesis of this book is that North Americans have now created a new language and imagery of death and grief, so as to overcome in part an earlier era's silence and denial. Since the early 1970s, an immense amount of "death and dying" literature has been written by secular and religious authors alike. Vehicles for its expression include autobiographical narratives, as well as "how to" guides for the dying, their caregivers, and the bereaved.

"Death is natural" is indeed one primary message of this new language. Such speech, as the widow learned, finds its home most securely within psychology, and carries with it the spiritual outlook of contemporary psychotherapies. Those who use it also sometimes see themselves as advocates on behalf of patients and their families, on behalf of all who feel powerless at the hands of a medicalized understanding of death. Its chief image for death is as "loss," and so mourning and the tasks of grieving become central concerns. But as the seminarian's remark reveals, it is sometimes appropriated wholeheartedly within the church. Christians have been challenged by its messages, discovering that what they heard or said *as Christians* made less sense than the newer message from psychological sources. Our goal is to learn how these latter have influenced Christian ways to encounter death, both theological and practical. What has happened to contemporary North American Christianity as a result of this influence?

For, to answer the question raised by the seminarian, yes, there is a lot more to say on the subject of death. Christians, in fact, have said an enormous amount, and "death is natural" is not prominent or even adequate as a summary of their meanings. The seminarian's dismissal of this tradition may have been informed and based on acute theological reflection; or it may have been a gut reaction to criticisms such as the widow's; or it may have been the response of one caught up in the appropriation of culturally plausible ideas, not yet able or willing to sort through their implications for Christian faith. But this task, I believe, is important not just for clergy and chaplains and those who work professionally with the dying and bereaved, but for all those who profess Christian faith and encounter death. This book will attempt to carry out some of the necessary examination, interpretation, and reflection, identifying areas of creative theological development and areas of conflict with traditional ways of identifying and resolving issues. To sharpen the focus and reveal what is at stake, each chapter includes a meditation on a scene from Jesus Christ's dying and death, which shows how the new perspectives illuminate but also conceal, and how they help make real meanings of the passion narrative in ways that were not possible or even permissable before. Yes, there is a lot to say on death, and what Christians say about the death of Jesus is connected (although not always clearly) with what we say about our own deaths.

But do we need another book on death and dying, on grief and bereavement? Aren't we faced with an abundance of resources on these topics, of "how to" books, spiritual guides to the perplexed, and solemn presentations of multistage models for coming to terms with loss? Yes, there is a lot of writing and speaking about dying and grief these days. Since the 1970s, Americans have become talkative about experiences they once kept secret and silent, such as the experiences of the dying and the bereaved. The helpful volumes of the 1970s are replaced by others, which either repeat the same advice or particularize it further. We no longer just have books for widows, but for young widows, young widows with children, and so forth. Moreover, in case theoretical self-help literature appears too impersonal, there are numerous autobiographical narratives on the same topics. These too began to appear in quantity in the 1970s (although there were a few instructive exceptions earlier), and new ones appear on bookstore shelves and in libraries every month. "How I coped with terminal illness" or "How I nursed my husband until his death" (yes, more are authored by women than by men) offer one person's experiences in lieu of generalized "how to" advice. Meanwhile, religious writers are hardly silent, and every religious publisher carries at least one "death and dying" title, either as a topic within pastoral care or as an inspirational work.

So why this book? I believe it is time to take stock, try to assess the new literature, and map its contours. I believe that what the death and dying literature says is relevant to people's lives. I am sure that the widow quoted at the start is not alone in her preference for the newer message over that associated with church and clergy. But this new language is not flawless and certainly is not complete. There are things said that have needed to be said, but also things about which we still hear nothing. To change our images, there are roads not taken, sometimes deliberately, sometimes without even seeing that they are there. Moreover, a minor underlying theme of much of this literature is a critique of what Christianity traditionally has had to say on the topics of dying, death, and grief. Or, to put this more cautiously, this literature presents a critique of what contemporary writers remember or reconstruct about what "traditional Christianity" used to say. This critique of Christianity is minor, in that it is far more muted than the critiques of secular, scientific North American medicine and its death-denying worldview, and of our society's continuing denial and repression of death. But Christians need a direct discussion of what seem to be points of conflict between the new voices on death and dying, in and out of the church, and Christianity's previous messages on the subject, especially if the seminarian, now long graduated, is still content to proclaim that "Death is natural" and cut off further conversation.

This goal means that I must stand back from the newer literature, and so risk sounding detached, nonautobiographical, and hands-off. Yet I am committed to making judgments and evaluations about the relative merits of different images and ideas. To some persons, this stance by its very nature seems inappropriate to the subject, as well as arrogant and judgmental. However, psychology and psychotherapies are never value-free. All therapies, be they ever so nonjudgmental, include a moral dimension. A discussion of "good grief" that contrasts it to "pathological grief" is as value-laden as any religious discussion of sin; both involve judgments about right and wrong, character virtues, and the human good. Although I believe that everyone has a story to tell, and each story is unique and valuable, this does not absolve me from the responsibility of making such judgments. In fact, the very claim that all stories are both unique and valuable rests on my high respect for individuality, the power of narrative, and the value of differences. I believe that the time has come to uncover, examine, and assess these assumptions. Those whose own work is hands-on daily caregiving, however, may be too immersed in their commitments and duties to engage in it. In addition, at a time when such drastic changes in the health care system are occurring, such reflections may seem beside the point, since social services such as bereavement counseling and chaplaincy programs are more vulnerable to cutbacks than other hospital activities. The real battle, advocates of such services will say, is the battle to save social and psychological care in the face of cost-cutting. If so, why offer a critique such as ours now? Won't it further undermine what needs to be strengthened?

This objection itself points to two remarkable features of the new death and dying literature. First, this literature tries to regain a human, personal, subjective dimension to the experience of illness, which the dominant model of Western medicine excludes. Western scientific medicine treats disease, provides acute care, and diagnoses using measures that largely bypass the patient's own report of symptoms. Its strengths lie in these areas. Medicine is weaker in dealing with chronic ailments, in palliative care, and in discovering how the patient's perspective is needed in the practice of the art of medicine.[1] As we will see, the bulk of the new literature on death and dying is focused upon medicalized dying, in hospitals or through hospice care at home. It is an advocacy literature, struggling to recognize the patient's experiences of illness, over against the dominance of the medical model. In spite of over two decades of hospice, and many legal changes supporting patients' rights to information and self-determination, this basic conflict remains and dominates public and private reflection on the experience of terminal illness and dying. The latest phase, over the financing of social services in an era of managed care, is part of this larger ongoing battle.

The second feature of the new death and dying literature is that it inherits the limited presuppositions of personality theory and insight-based psychotherapies. Psychotherapy names emotions and maps the hidden contours of inner life with great sensitivity and complexity. Yet it is culturally bound, privatized, to some extent class bound, and favors people who are educated, articulate, introspective. Counselors and theorists are not unaware of these limits, and have tried to overcome them. Typically, however, they first formulate issues in terms that make sense to educated, middle-class North Americans (assumed to be of European background and therefore "white"), then they modify these ideas for applications to other groups. "How to" works may assume their readers belong to the educated middle-class population, but authors sometimes explicitly add that the same practices may not work, for example, within the Korean-American community, or in working-class families. It is important to recognize these limits and differences. But the intrinsic universal quality of psychological language makes such strategies seem like afterthoughts. The autobiographies that have focused on illness and grief do not provide a counterweight, since their educated upper-middle-class narrators by and large reflect the same values and ideals of the psychological theorists. Few who are not of Northern European background write full-length "how I coped with terminal illness" tales. I find no such autobiographies written by residents of my blue-collar neighborhood of South Philadelphia, or any place like it. People of Mediterranean background generally do not write them, nor do Korean Americans, African Americans, or Puerto Ricans.[2]

I know that for some of this book's potential readers, these drawbacks are already substantial. For them, both the death and dying literature and my analysis of it will be nothing but replications of the inequalities and biases of North American culture. But this is a shortsighted response. Consider the era of silence and denial that immediately preceded the current rediscovery of dying and grief, which historian Philippe Ariès has termed, the time of "wild death." Looking at France at mid-century, he found the same silence and denial that North Americans and British also endured. "I do not mean that death had once been wild," says Ariès. "I mean, on the contrary, it has become wild."[3] "Wild" is outside of any language or meaning, unknown and terrifying. For many Americans, the code word for this era is "the '50s." Such people remember this era as "off the scale in denial" (in the words of Paul Monette) on other matters too; they recall school exercises of hiding under desks in case of atomic attack. Denial of death is a complex process that includes many defense mechanisms, specific illness-behaviors, and impairments of realistic thought. But in popular perception, the '50s mark the highest level of blatant and simplistic denial. In the decades since 1970, new words have been spoken and new images created; this represents in itself a major accomplishment. When we look back, we can gauge both how far we have come, and how far we still need to go to distance ourselves from what the '50s represent.

This development of new words and images is also a religious innovation at the level of faith and spirit. I believe that this religious innovation has been insufficiently recognized, perhaps because pastoral counselors, chaplains, and other clergy have been busy learning the psychological perspectives. Clergy should not merely echo these, but try to theologize in response to them. Meanwhile, a growing interest in spirituality has blurred many familiar boundaries between psychology and religion. Today many persons speak of a spiritual dimension to dying, loss, and grief, even if the exact words used are not from an established religious tradition. I find that in such usage, "spirituality" becomes a "glow word," filled with positive feelings, but lacking exact definition. Sometimes it is used to mean the private, personal side of one's formal religion. This is the most time-sanctioned meaning (as in phrases such as "Eucharistic spirituality"). But today, spirituality may designate a "depth dimension," present if unnoticed within all human experience, something close to what theologian Paul Tillich called "faith" almost fifty years ago. It may be used to emphasize the nonmaterial dimension of human beings as unique individuals. None of these definitions are wrong, but they are not identical in scope or intention. Some who refer to spirituality today include reference to a "Higher Power." This testimony to twelve-step programs also expresses the hope that we can find a generic spirituality beyond all particulars, which will nevertheless include some particular content. It is significant that the term "spirituality" itself fills a niche today, and whether in spite of or because its definitions are so broad and vague, it is exceedingly popular.

For purposes of this book, I wish to reduce this confusion and offer a working definition of spirituality. Spirituality is what for humans evokes, suggests, or points toward ultimacy, a quality or dimension of many perspectives on death, in and out of historical traditions. A more formal definition includes both an outward and inward face for spirituality.

> Facing outward, human existence is spiritual insofar as it engages reality as a maximally inclusive whole and makes the cosmos an intentional object of thought and feeling. Facing inward, life has a spiritual dimension to the extent that it is apprehended as a project of one's most enduring and vital self.[4]

"Religion" will be reserved for traditional communities of faith, even when these are relatively new on the North American scene. Religion is a matter of community, of shared and transmitted beliefs, values, and practices.

Yet this book will treat both "religion" as well as "spirituality." We will note how grief and mourning are now marked as topics of relevance to Christians, to theology even, as they were not in the past. We will note how contemporary Christian treatment of various death-related themes drops some ideas totally, employs others sparingly, and disagrees on what in the past went unquestioned. Much of this revisioning has happened rather silently. It seems to cross theological boundaries such as Protestant and Roman Catholic, conservative and liberal, so that it is not a case of two sides lining up behind competing ideological banners. Unlike debates about abortion and homosexuality, which have been public, loud, and acrimonious in and out of churches, some theological shifts have proceeded smoothly and quietly. Take, for example, the question of divine impassibility. The very fact that hardly anyone recognizes this term proves the quiet change. Impassibility is the condition of being invulnerable to suffering. If everything living comes into existence, experiences limits and changes, and then decays and dies, the same is not true of God. While we are weak and mortal, God is not. While we are influenced by time, place, social prejudices, the limits of our minds, and our biochemistry, God is not. We are dim, flickering candles; God is the Sun. Our lives are built on sand and tides; God is the Eternal Rock. Traditional attributes of God included impassibility, and as all these images suggest, it signifies immunity from what makes human life messy and miserable. In God, purity, permanence, and transcendence of pain could be secured, because God himself carried these qualities.

This view is dominant no longer. In twentieth-century theology and pastoral writings, divine impassibility has been abandoned in favor of an image of God who suffers with us and for us.[5] No longer are the images of impassibility treasured as signs of transcendence; they instead appear as mistaken efforts to detach God from the sorrow and travail of creation, as the God of the Bible never would wish to be. The biblical God is anything but impassible in the face of his people's sins, exile, and suffering; he anguishes over them, as a betrayed spouse (Hosea) or a parent (Isaiah). Above all, Jesus shows God as suffering and dying and redeeming a sinful, murderous world. A God who was truly impassible would not have cared enough to create, let alone to save human beings. A God who suffers is a God who cares, and if we know that God cares, then God could not be untouched by suffering. Thus, divine impassibility is inadequate theology, and the idea itself has vanished from contemporary Christian writings. Indeed, contemporary debates and critiques of the parent and spouse imagery, focused on issues of gender, nowhere condemn the motif of divine suffering, and have no interest in returning us to a vision of impassibility. One dimension of these debates, in fact, may be the inability of the traditional masculine imagery (in the eyes of some critics) to adequately convey care, moving us all completely beyond impassibility and its detachment from empathy with pain.

Not all examples are so neat; not all seem so removed from the publicized areas of controversy. But we will find that forgotten choices, hidden shifts of meaning, and deliberate substitution of new images for old, fill our story. We have a new language for dying and death, and it has reshaped how we use the old. As we will see in turning to the dying of Jesus, this new language lets us read an old text afresh, making accessible what earlier generations may have missed. For although the secular culture of the "wild death" era may have said nothing and gotten away with that, Christianity never had the option of total silence. Yet as a resource for contemporary persons in their quests for meaning and community in the face of dying, death, and grief, Christianity has proved an ambiguous and frequently disappointing source. As the divine impassibility example shows, beliefs once intended to provide encouragement and hope can appear wretchedly unhelpful to later generations. The widow who expressed frustration with whatever the church and its representatives said to her, in contrast to the believable and hopeful message that "death is natural," is not an isolated or atypical figure. Some of what was done in the past should never have been done at all, and we should be grateful that it has either disappeared or is on the way to being replaced by something better. However, what distinguishes any discussions on dying, death, and grief from discussions about Christianity and gender or sexuality issues, is a level of humility on the part of contemporary participants. Our society may know more about the causes and prevention of disease than the people of the past, but we know less about death as a human situation. We are more bereft of wisdom here—tragically so—than even communities who in other ways we might find primitive or ignorant. Good ideas from the past, or from outside the boundaries of our society, ought therefore to be welcomed by us as possibilities even if we do not finally accept them.

When we start looking for resources in our quest to understand and deal with death, however, we should be very careful for two reasons. First, we risk using our own standard of "helpfulness" uncritically and jettisoning images and ideas that may balance or correct our own partial vision. In an astonishingly short time, these jettisoned ideas and images can be rediscovered, rescued, and made resources once again in ways that no one could have predicted. A vivid example of this is the topic of angels, their reality and special functions. About twenty years ago, Stephen Crites wrote an essay in a volume on theology and storytelling entitled "Angels We Have Heard" in which he focused on angels as those who invite us into stories. "'Angel' was the name we chose to signify a narrative ambiguity," he declared.[6] The author admitted that this topic betrayed his eccentricity, his bizarre if imaginative playfulness. Most readers must have found it enjoyable as fantasy, but outrageous as serious religious thought. Today, Crites' essay would barely astonish anyone, because he nowhere argues that angels exist outside of "narrative ambiguity," nor does he include any contemporary tales of persons guided or guarded by angels. Our tolerance for discourse about angels has altered dramatically, even among those of us who have never seen one, or who doubt that they are very significant even if they might in some sense exist as more than a special way to name "narrative ambiguity." Angels have appeared on the Christmas covers of both major weekly newsmagazines, precisely because they have become a resource for religious imagination and appropriation once again. Perhaps this change is an example of theological "dumbing down," guided by media and greeting cards rather than by improved religious sensitivities, but it surely suggests how tentative any assessments of what "secular persons" can swallow must be, and how judgments about the potential resources of the past need to be made with humility.

A second reason for caution lies in the image of "resources" itself. The term, for me at least, connotes the quest for oil and coal and natural gas, a quest intimately tied to colonialism and multinational capitalism. (The oil in Saudi Arabia was under the desert when Muhammad and his followers rode over it, but it was not a resource for them.) The vision of the natural world as potential "resources" turns land into real estate, forests into timber, rivers into sources of electric power. This same vision, when turned toward intangible, spiritual "resources," may appropriate the traditions of other peoples in a parallel, distorting, and self-interested manner, without asking their permission. Appropriation may be based on admiration, envy, and respect for what such peoples retain that we have lost and desperately need, but this is, or can become, a kind of spiritual colonialism of which we should be wary. Although the particular examples most often cited are the spiritual resources of native peoples, the same could be true for the practices and beliefs of Christians living in cultures on the margins of the postindustrial world. In what sense do traditional Spanish-American Day of the Dead ceremonies become resources for us, when few of us participate in their culture or lifestyle? As we will see, nostalgia for the death and bereavement practices of small-scale traditional societies permeates the newer death and dying literature. It is common to find portraits of Day of the Dead types of rituals introduced for contrast, to illustrate how modern society and its mourners suffer when denuded of meaningful public rites. Even when authors are too cautious to suggest direct appropriation of others' rituals, their rhetoric of nostalgia encourages borrowings and appropriations as solutions to the problem of ritual and symbolic emptiness. Current criticism of enthusiastic borrowing from exotic spiritual sources differs from more familiar concern over syncretism. Christianity—indeed all historical religious traditions—may be itself a product of mixing and blending several religious cultures, and thus syncretistic from its very early days. But some mixes are ludicrously mismatched, and will never work. Stephen Levine's example of the woman who wished to read her dying Jewish mother excerpts from the *Tibetan Book of the Dead* is instructive as to how even someone thoroughly eclectic will find it advisable to limit the borrowing to what will actually make sense to the persons most in need. In this case, he suggested, traditional Yiddish folktales could comfort the elderly mother far more than an exotic Buddhist text of the soul's adventures after death.[7]

Perhaps a more open-minded and more generous way to approach this question of borrowing, appropriation, and resources, is to admit that a vacuum existed, if not for everyone then for many of us. A whole society with no public language to speak in the face of death, illness, and grief— except the language of medicine and disease—is desperate for meaning. The situation of "wild death" and its silence was not bearable. The words needed came not from communal rituals, nor from theology, nor from scientific empiricism. They are not merely the words of experts, but the words of sufferers intertwined with those of counselors and caregivers who become advocates of the dying and bereaved. Part of what makes this new development so exciting is the voicing of what had not been spoken before, of going into territory unknown and unmarked. This makes dying and mourning much more difficult than in settings where there is one pattern that everyone knows and is obligated to follow. But it offers space for new meanings, for the process of creating rather than imitating a preset model. As Cathy Davidson, writing on the death of her mother-in-law, finds: "We've never been taught the words for this farewell. We find words all our own."[8] If any words from the past, from traditions, from anywhere, can be made resources for us, they will not become substitutes for speaking words all our own. The new language of dying and death and grief will be strengthened, but we must still, today, here, do the speaking.

The new language is still in the process of being shaped. It is definitely beyond silence and denial, but it is not fixed or frozen. I believe that we can examine its contributions and its gaps, allowing that it may be more changeable and more varied as time goes by. As Christians use this new language and our visions and voices echo and modify it, we may be able to find its weak places and its oversights, and respond to these constructively. This is the hope and aim of this book.

I

The Roles of Death
in Christian Faith

This book contrasts old with new, then with now, what was formerly the norm for language about death with the emerging norms of contemporary North America. In this format, one could easily paint a convenient caricature of the old ways, a vision of traditional Christianity as it once was, to set over against the way things are now. Two such caricatured versions already exist, and are already common in the writings relevant to this topic. But if we want to answer the question, "Is death necessarily an important topic for Christianity, and if so, why and how?" we will have to move beyond both of them.

What are the twin caricatures? The first is of a hellfire and brimstone religion of fear, where everyone devalued this life, concentrated on avoiding Hell, and became fixated on details of Purgatory, the Last Judgment, and anything except daily life in this world here and now. Christianity trashes this world, for the sake of a dim and pale Heaven, and with an obscene fascination for the torments of Hell. We have built such a picture from nightmarish artistic renderings of sinners' punishments and from texts of sermons warning of impending apocalypse. Our assumption is that everyone in medieval times truly feared, truly believed, was truly captured in the web of fear spun by the church. Accordingly, any really solvable problems these people faced went unsolved, precisely because their eyes were watching a hellish future and turned away from ordinary life. So firmly is this portrait set in many of our minds, that it is easier to construct an alternative "pure religion of love" preached by Jesus (nineteenth-century liberal Protestant theologies did just this) than it is to question if medieval persons actually took Hell so seriously, so personally, as our imaginative portrait assumes. Perhaps they did, but perhaps they assumed that Hell was for other people. Perhaps a sermon on apocalypse was entertainment to them, closer to a horror movie than to existential dread. Public disbelief about such matters was not permitted, but private scepticism—or at least a pervasive assumption that Hell was for other, "really evil" persons—may have been much more widespread than we have assumed.[1] Still, the portrait of traditional Christianity as a religion of fear, exclusively otherworldly, retains a hold on contemporary persons. Sometimes even a brief reminder of it is enough to remind spiritually vacillating persons why they dropped out of church.

The other caricature goes something like this: the dying grandmother lies in her own bed, surrounded by several generations of her family. A few days before, she knew her time was growing short, so the word went out to the whole village to come pay final goodbyes to a beloved and irreplaceable member of the community. Everyone was welcome and, true to her character, she was always more concerned with the comfort and health of her visitors than with her own pain. Now the pastor enters to offer her companionship and spiritual comfort. The consolation of religion is that soon she will be home with the Lord. She tells the pastor that she can sense the presence of angels around her. "I am certain of my soul's salvation," she insists as he offers her the assurance that "The Lord is with you now." She is genuinely joyful at her approaching death, and, hearing distant heavenly music, she hums gently. Her death, when it comes, is peaceful and leaves everyone with a sense of triumph, of a journey well completed. Yes, they are bereaved and will miss her. But they know that she is with the Lord, and that they will join her one day. This is what the phrase "that old time religion" most commonly evokes for many contemporary Americans, a religion that felt true and certain, that helped prepare persons for death without exiling them from this life and their loved ones.

This second picture is more frequently found in the contemporary literature on death and dying than the first. It combines the comfort of Heaven with the remembrance of the community. That the most prevalent form of Anglo-American "old time religion"—the Wesleyan Methodism that advocated a model of "happy dying"—began in urban slums among the poor and dispossessed, is unintegrated into the above portrayal. Similarly, it is an unremembered element in the scene above that about four out of ten children would be joining Grandma in Heaven long before they reached adolescence. Even the pastor's role was not, strictly speaking, to bring comfort, but to address the question, "How is your soul in relation to God?" The dying sinner did not receive consolation or empathy, but was offered a last chance to repent. The casebook of a nineteenth-century pastoral counselor used by Seward Hiltner for his own mid-twentieth-century writings on pastoral care makes this clear.[2]

To begin to answer the question, "What is the role of death in Christian faith?" in a more balanced and nuanced way, we must set aside both of these portraits. They are powerful, there are reasons why they are credible, and reasons why we cling to them. But historical truth is more complicated than either suggests. Moreover, Christian thought makes other connections not addressed in either portrayal. Even looking directly at visions of the self's death from past eras, we can find that there is much more to say. Not all of it can be said here. Because this is a book by a North American Protestant, the focus will be on forms of Christianity relevant to that context. Today we are more aware than ever before of the great diversity of Christian practice and devotional piety, and are more reluctant to conclude that anything is "sub-Christian" just because it is different. Think, for example, of Ethiopians whose faith centers upon their most sacred relic, the ark of the covenant, not "lost," as in the Steven Spielberg movie, but given by King Solomon to the Queen of Sheba as she returned home to bear his son, according to their traditions. For them, Christian faith has a different landscape.

Christians have always said about death that Jesus died and rose from the dead. Christ's death is the core of the passion narrative that became the framework for the four canonical gospels. His death, the events leading up to his death, his teachings that provoked the authorities to arrest him, his awareness of his own end: these became the treasured memories and traditions of the early Christian communities, and were written down to proclaim the meaning of his death for all peoples. Moreover, in Christian baptism, we are all participants in his death. This death is described as a sacrifice, an atonement for sin, a way to effect redemption and the triumph over death itself. In raising Jesus up from death, God vindicated him, God triumphed over death's dominion, and henceforth God promised new and eternal life to all who believe. Does resurrection reverse the death, or does it complete what Christ's life and his death portray? Is his death shame and the resurrection glory, or is the death itself his glorification? These questions set the field of the narrative, whose details are thoroughly intertwined with theological motifs. When Jesus cries out from the cross, "My God, my God, why have you forsaken me?" he allows the readers and hearers to enter into a vision of God, death, and separation that is also the ending of death as we have known or assumed it to be. "It is finished," he says. A new relationship to God, to death, and to ourselves is now possible.

I begin here, and in a sense never wish to leave this starting place. Of course, there are forms of Christianity focused elsewhere, such as on creation or on the Holy Spirit as a force or power coming later at Pentecost. But of Mark's sixteen chapters, eight deal with the final week of Jesus' life; Paul claims that he taught and knows nothing but "Christ crucified." Following this, the Christian faith has always in its sacramental, ritual life focused on "remembering Christ's death until he comes," in its celebration of Holy Communion. Salvation, redemption, justification, atonement: these are some of the theological metaphors for what God accomplished through the death of Jesus the Christ. Based on what is in Paul's letters, his converts might never have learned that Jesus taught in parables, but they heard from the start that he died "for our sins" on the cross.

Moreover, if the letters of Ignatius (c.110 A.D.) represent a typical development of the ancient church, fascination with death, eternal life, immortality, and martyrdom shines through as the appeal of the new religion. True, not every early Christian died a martyr, or knew long in advance that he or she would be martyred. But in the spirituality of Ignatius, the sacraments have become "the medicine of immortality," and themes of violent death as the mode of identification with Christ are set to influence the church long after. This vision sets in motion, among other things, fascination with the deaths, graves, and remains of the martyrs themselves, which became a means to link not only the living and the blessed dead, but the far-flung dioceses of the church on earth. Gifts and exchanges of martyrs' bones were, as Peter Brown shows,[3] not just an accidental concession to "popular superstition" but a definite, central policy to establish connections as political units floundered and were violently destroyed.

Martyrdom became transformed into an ascetic "white martyrdom" after the establishment of Christianity as the official religion of the Roman Empire. In other words, when joining Christ in his death no longer meant finding oneself in the arena ready to be torn apart by wild beasts (Ignatius really looked forward to this violent destruction of his body), another way to identify with Christ's passion and death emerged. Individual men and women, especially in Egypt, became "dead" to the world and to their ordinary identities, preferring a life beyond the boundaries of human society. In the desert, in caves and trees, and even perched on pillars, they struggled to attain that state of transfigured new life of the resurrection, while still within the bodies and limits of this existence. In their best insights, they recognized how impossible this aim was: one never in this life became totally free of the body or of sin. One fought a hidden fight, no longer against wild beasts of the arena but against the wild imaginings of one's own soul. The strange (to us) lives of these people reveal an intense involvement with salvation as a process of deep purification and self-knowledge; the real desert and wilderness are revealed as this inner landscape of the hidden always-sinful soul.

Naturally, the average Christian of these centuries was neither a martyr nor a desert ascetic. But the models of strenuous heroic striving after death-in-life were so powerful that baptism itself became problematic. How could anyone live free from domination by sin? Perhaps it was the domination by church leaders that really worried them, but many active persons, particularly men in public life, preferred to postpone baptism until they were near death. "Too weak to commit any more serious sins, they bring their dying bodies to God" church leaders complained repeatedly. Baptism shifted for a time from a rite of sharing in Christ's death to one that served as the viaticum out of this life itself. This was also the case for dying infants and children, who in those days were not normally baptized immediately. We know of at least one case where the pious grandmother insisted that the dying baby receive baptism "so that he might depart from the world as a believer."[4] This was not looked on as objectionable, in contrast to the baptism of dying adults who had postponed the rite. Eventually, when baptism of infants became the norm, the rite lost most of its associations with death altogether, and became linked with "new birth" into the spiritual and social orders.

Note that I have said nothing directly about the afterlife. Did the martyrs expect to join Christ in Paradise? Yes, just as Stephen received a vision of his Lord just on the brink of his own death (Acts 7:55–56). What did others anticipate? Would they "sleep" until awakened at the day of judgment? Did they restlessly require the assistance of the living for their continuing purification? We know that all of these expectations were voiced, but for the first thousand years of Western Christianity vagueness and diffuseness remained the norm. Answers to the question, "What becomes of me personally after death?" were not intensely nor universally sought, as they would become in a later era. This absence of fixation on one's own dying has struck historian Philippe Ariès; he speaks of "tame death" for this period, as if dying were like moving to the house next door. Although this view may have been true to the manner in which ordinary persons faced their deaths, it is a mistake to generalize to the level of religious thought. Theologically, death was not so tame. Ancient and medieval beliefs in Purgatory, prayers for intercession by martyrs and saints, and a general sense that Christianity provides the remedy for death, meant that death was not "natural," not taken so matter-of-factly, as the "tame death" model seems to suggest to us. If we concentrate on Western, Latin Christianity, whose primary architects were Augustine and Gregory the Great, we may see that issues around sin, atonement, and penance became absolutely central in a way that, apparently, they were not earlier on, or in other cultural areas. The link between death and punishment for sin was made firmer and stronger, although that link is certainly found in Paul's letter to the Romans. How salvation, justification, and paying the penalty for sin all fit together set Christian theology on a track that eventually made unambiguous definitions and explicit doctrinal formulations on these topics the hope for all parties. Even if we take a well-loved early medieval document, Bede's *History of the English Church and People* (written in the eighth century), we can see these issues shaping up. Bede's history concentrates on the period after Augustine (not of Hippo) brings monks to Canterbury on the pope's orders to attempt the conversion of the English peoples. We are never given a clear picture of what they believed before their conversion, but in one of the book's memorable scenes, a local pagan priest tells his king in the presence of all the counselors and the monks:

> Your majesty, when we compare the present life of man on earth with that time of which we have no knowledge, it seems to me like the swift flight of a single sparrow through the banqueting-hall where you are sitting at dinner on a winter's day with your thanes and counsellors. In the midst there is a comforting fire to warm the hall; outside, the storms of winter rain or snow are raging. This sparrow flies swiftly in through one door of the hall and out through another. While he is inside, he is safe from the winter storms; but after a few moments of comfort, he vanishes from sight into the wintry world from which he came. Even so, man appears on earth for a little while; but of what went before this life or of what follows, we know nothing. Therefore, if this new teaching has brought any more certain knowledge, it seems only right that we should follow it.[5]

Life before birth was never a Christian topic, but how to reframe the fate of human beings after death so to transform the picture itself was indeed what the new teaching could offer. There is other evidence in Bede's book that making sense of death, and indeed, how to deal with death and the dead, was an intrinsic part of the new religion's appeal. Critics might point out that Bede is a Christian author, telling his story from the perspective of Christianity's triumph. Those who accept the negative caricature of Christianity as an otherworldly, fear-driven faith will claim that its real impact was to reverse the values of the pagan universe, so that the warm banqueting hall of this life became a kind of wintry snowstorm, with the sparrow progressing toward fulfillment outside the hall's walls. However, if this speech is at all a valid representation of early medieval British thought, it suggests how the sense of mystery and menace surrounding individual death was indeed a key ingredient in how the new religion was received.

It was not fascination with the afterlife in itself, but the promise of some link between living and dead that apparently made Purgatory so central to Western piety in the High Middle Ages. Jacques LeGoff's *The Birth of Purgatory* shows how increasing fascination with the exact locale, the exact punishments, the exact durations of one's stay in Purgatory, led the Roman Catholic Church into a literalism and doctrinal specificity that the Eastern Orthodox churches found outlandish and bizarre. Where was Purgatory? Who went there? By what mechanisms could their time be shortened? How literally did its flames burn? Le Goff tries to show how these questions went together with a recognition that human society, justice, and blame, were all more complex than people had previously supposed.[6] This affected the criminal justice systems of the time, as well as eschatological imagery. A vague division between the good and the wicked, the sheep and the goats, was insufficient for a society that really needed to deal comprehensively with issues of responsibility, guilt, and punishment. Few of us are obvious saints, few of us really believe we deserve the fires of eternal Hell. For the morally intermediate majority, Purgatory became a way to think through and evaluate the quality of their lives.

Sometimes these verdicts could undermine the official teachings of the church, as when a widow whose dead husband had made his living by usury (we would say "loan-sharking") claimed that he was in Purgatory and in need of redeeming prayers and masses. Purgatory was a place from which there was eventual release, but usury was a sin that officially was so serious that to make one's living from it guaranteed one a place in Hell. Normally, although Purgatory linked the living and the dead, it did so in a way that made the church its broker.

Dante's *Divine Comedy* fixed high medieval beliefs so firmly that these became dominant images of what Hell, Purgatory, and Paradise really are like. The pains of the Inferno are unending and profitless; those who suffer them can never truly repent or be rehabilitated, but will only sink deeper into despair, self-pity, and bitterness. There is no solidarity in sin; even the pitiful lovers joined together in their torment are severed from real communion. Whether despairing and pitiful, like the anonymous suicide whose soul is trapped in a tree and can only speak when the leaves are torn and bleed, or whether defiant, like the giant heretic who lies in a burning coffin shouting blasphemies at God, these people map out limits to human evil. Dante visits them to recognize and reject evil in himself. In contrast, Purgatory's pains have some purpose; they are rehabilitative more than they are retributive. Those inhabitants of Purgatory with whom he speaks include "the late penitent," and some whose actual lives were much worse than many of the Inferno dwellers. The mercy of God makes this possible, so that a focus on justice is at least partly balanced by recognition that the outward reputation of a life is not the same as its final inward turning. On that final disposition God relies, making one's last moments count more decisively than they might have otherwise. As for the blessed in Paradise, at one point the poet tells us that they can no longer remember or think of sin, so purified are they from its powers, but then he promptly violates this in order to have them converse at all. However, prophecies and fulminations about the evils of the rulers and people of Florence (from which city Dante was in exile when he wrote the *Divine Comedy*) eventually cease, as he and his celestial guide Beatrice rise higher into Paradise's upper spheres. Righteous indignation, like pride in one's ancestry, is permissible in Heaven, but its cause appears too squalid to be worth fussing about as the most holy reaches of the blessed are achieved. Significantly, there is a cross even in Paradise; the realm of Mars, where the great warriors of God dwell (crusaders, including a putative ancestor of the poet), is centrally lighted by a red-toned cross, whose "thousand points of light" are themselves the souls of the dead. Those who are true warriors of God share the link with Christ's death, even at the highest, most death-free level of things. The cross is not left behind; Christ's passion and death have some place and meaning even here.

Readers today find in this poem a complete map of human existence, or a Jungian-style journey of the soul through its own depths into its own further transcendent reaches. We do not worry if any of our relatives and associates are among those the poet consigned to Hell. Nor do we find in the poem an answer to the question, "Where is the entrance to Purgatory?" for which various suggested locales (Ireland, Sicily) had been offered. (By locating Mt. Purgatory on the far side of the earth, Dante avoided the known geography of his time.) It is also possible for us to notice how the poet himself empathizes and shows contempt for various categories of sinners, following sensitivities that do not always mirror church teachings. His pity for the suicides and the sodomites contrasts greatly to his scorn and hatred of the grafters and usurers, for instance, although the locations for all these people follow the Aristotelian moral scheme which had become official code.

Shortly after Dante's death in 1321 came the Black Death, years of plague which reduced the population of Western Europe by about one-third. Although we understand the medical mechanisms behind this disease, during the fourteenth century people knew it was dreadfully contagious and quickly fatal. In less than a day, one could go from feeling perfectly fit to being gruesomely sick and then dead. Part of the horror of this kind of mass death was, and remains, that ordinary burial and mourning was impossible; anonymity, impersonality, and a kind of brutal numbing out marked the deaths that overtook people in this and other epidemics. However, it is well to remember that most burials in those days were anonymous anyway. There was no cult of individual memorials for ordinary folk, and so no standard tending of their gravesites by families. Unless you were a very famous person, you got buried along with everyone else, and sooner or later your bones were dug up to make room for those of the newly dead. Nevertheless, the suddenness of the plague, its mysterious spread, and the absolute helplessness of people to treat its symptoms led to a new and increased fascination with individual death.

Out of this experience of mass death came the *Ars Moriendi,* the "art of dying" literature. These were treatises put together for the dying person who might not have a priest at hand to perform sacramental actions for him or her. *The Book of the Craft of Dying* is a self-help guide for the dying and their friends, to meet the temptations peculiar to the dying state, and to prepare for what comes after death. This literature was so popular that it survived the Reformation in Protestant countries, and continued to be reprinted well into the early modern period. Later examples, such as Jeremy Taylor's *Holy Dying* (1651) and Robert Bellamine's *The Art of Dying Well* (1619) build on the simpler, anonymous works that constitute a tradition of "how to" literature on individual dying.

What is the view of death, faith, God, and self in this literature? It corresponds neither to the negative caricature—there is no portrayal of the flames of Hell—nor to the positive, idealized consolation and comfort model. Although some Stoic language of "life as an evil, death as a release from it" is offered, the most dominant theme is that dying is a difficult, painful process that offers special temptations and special challenges to the soul. These begin with the temptation to abandon faith, a foundation upon which one's whole worldview rests. Another temptation is denial, refusal to admit that death is near (remembering the symptoms of the plague, "near" may have meant "in a few hours"), for which the remedy is the realism of the friend or companion who reads the book to or with the dying. "Death is near; turn your attention away from what distracts you from that" is the message. The other temptations are impatience, including anger at God for the physical suffering of one's illness; despair over one's unconfessed sins, and complacency or pride in oneself and one's moral accomplishments. These five bear an uncanny resemblence to the contemporary schema of "five stages of dying," not in any sense of a sequence, nor in their exact content, but in the underlying concern with the inner experiences of an individual facing an ultimate crisis point in their existence.

Each temptation has its specific remedy (as in all self-help literature). It is noteworthy that the solution to unconfessed sins and the despair these bring is that God is always ready to forgive.

> Therefore should no man despair . . . for though any one man or woman had done as many thefts, or manslaughters, or as many other sins as be drops of water in the sea, and gravel stones in the strand, though he had never done penance for them afore, nor never had been shriven of them before . . . yet should he never despair; for in such a case very contrition of heart within, with will to be shriven if time sufficed, is sufficient and accepted by God for to save him everlastingly.[7]

Thus, unequivocably, at the brink of death, salvation by faith in divine mercy supersedes any focus on merits or works, and indeed the sacramental function of the priest is not absolutely necessary either. These books could therefore survive among both Protestants and Roman Catholics, and continue to play their role of guiding individuals out of this life into the next.

That transition is what their model of death is based upon. Death is not a loss or an emotional separation from family. In fact, the family plays no role in the drama, and attachments to them and to occupations in the world are distractions. This is made clearer in the late medieval woodcut that serves as the frontispiece in the reissued version of *The Book of the Craft of Dying*. Here a dying man is surrounded by Christ on the cross, by saints, and demons. An angel holds a curtain between this scene and two ordinary human figures, representing the family members. The real drama excludes them, it is a supernatural encounter, not a natural event. Nor is dying in any way a medical event; the doctor is not part of the scene, part of the dialogues, part of anything. The specific disease of the body is entirely irrelevant, a view difficult for many of us to grasp. Death is a spiritual ultimate weighing of one's soul and one's existence by God. Overall, what will happen at death is that the soul will meet God, and in this meeting the real meaning and worth of one's life will be revealed. This vision of death as awesome and ultimate makes everything else seem trivial. Even fascination with the details of Purgatory, which is the assumed destination of all readers of *Ars Moriendi,* is excluded.

What truly can aid the dying person on the brink of this encounter with God? It is Christ's dying that can serve as a model and a consolation here, says the anonymous author. As a model, Christ did five things on the cross: he prayed, he cried, he wept, he commended his soul to God, and he gave up his spirit willingly.[8] We too should cry and weep to God for forgiveness of our sins, although how these tears of our repentance might be relevant to the sinless Christ the author of *The Book of the Craft of Dying* does not explore. Christ is also a consolation, for behold "the disposition of Christ in the cross":

> Take heed and see: His head is inclined to salve thee; His mouth to kiss thee; His arms spread to embrace thee; His hands pleased to give thee; His side opened to love thee; His body along strait to give all Himself to thee.[9]

Here Christ becomes the blessed, welcoming presence, whose own dying body becomes almost maternal in its love for the dying soul. Christ is both a moral example in his dying and a divine lover, whose very physicalness is a reminder of God's wonderful love for those who share in his passion.

Why pay so much attention to this odd text? Because it was genuinely popular and, unlike the official teachings, it is clear that what was said here would not have been repeated over and over again for so many centuries if it had not meant a great deal to ordinary persons. True, Christians even in Western Europe could live and die without sharing this intense preoccupation with personal dying. Moreover, there were Christians outside Western

Europe—in the Near East and India, for example—for whom this kind of preoccupation would have been foreign. The reason for this was not because they were more secular, but because the forms that their faith took did not make death, atonement, and penance such central issues. It may be that their contributions to contemporary North American Christianity lie in the future, and that it is from such sources that a new Christian language of dying and death could emerge. But until then, the story I am telling is that of the tradition, of the old language, and this is shaped by *Ars Moriendi* and its preoccupations, where the drama of the individual mortal self is already central.

What the Reformation brought was not the introduction of individualism, which was there already, but the elimination of Purgatory and the church's role in linking the living and the dead. As a result of financial abuses, Purgatory was viewed as a moneymaking, postbiblical distortion, and completely rejected by all branches of Protestants. In bitter Reformation polemics, those church leaders who raised funds by publicizing Purgatory were labelled *Totenfresser,* "the devourers of the dead."[10] Perhaps this anger, similar to contemporary accusations against the funeral industry, was present long before Luther, but the Reformation allowed for it to be vented for the first time. Whatever the differences between Anglicans and the Reformed, between Lutherans and Mennonites on topics such as the sacraments, infant baptism, and the relation between the visible church (the actual institution) and the invisible (the community of the elect or saved), all of these groups rejected an intermediate destination for the dead. Moreover, once the dead were either with God in Heaven or apart from God in Hell, there was no point praying for them, let alone to them. In that sense, they dropped out of the picture. In official Protestant teachings, they have remained out of the picture. This is not to say that care of graves became any worse or any better; that seems to have been a fluctuating matter, and whatever individualism Protestantism encouraged did not immediately produce individual, marked gravesites for everyone.

However, it may have produced an increased sense of anxiety about the "marks" of election, given how loosened were the connections between one's deeds (and the "merits" that no longer accumulated any theological status) and one's ultimate destiny. The most publicized modern account of this distinctively Protestant anxiety is Max Weber's thesis in *The Protestant Ethic and the Spirit of Capitalism* that anxiety over one's individual salvation gave rise to ever-more-intense efforts to succeed in one's vocation, to prove to oneself and others that God had truly created one among the elect. This aspect of Weber's overall interpretation is also the most frequently criticized. But what he noted was a pattern of emphasis on long-term, "innerworldly asceticism" as the model of moral life, rather than on isolated good deeds. Weber's Puritans (for he is speaking not of the first generations of Reformers, but their descendents) work hard, live frugally, consider themselves stewards of their goods rather than enjoyers of their wealth, and consistently maintain a pattern of rational, calculated planned activity. These stand in contrast to some of Dante's inhabitants of lower Paradise who lived loose, reckless lives but secretly supported hermits, and so by their occasional charitable acts, not to mention the fervent prayers of their relatives, overcame a dubious lifestyle. Does this "innerworldly asceticism" truly make persons more fearful, more anxious, more insecure, more worried about their own proximity to Hell? It is easy to cite Jonathan Edwards' (in)famous sermon, "Sinners in the Hands of an Angry God," to support such a thesis, but this address was unusual enough to spark a religious revival, the First Great Awakening. Moreover, its enormous impact on young persons seems to have been intensified by a local string of early deaths, shocking frivolous teenagers into awareness of mortality.

The best evidence of the preoccupation with one's own salvation is the extraordinary seriousness with which some people took life's journey as a constant series of dangers, temptations, and gateways down to Hell. This helps account for the long-term and widespread popularity of John Bunyan's *The Pilgrim's Progress*. No account of Christian perspectives on death written for English-speaking North Americans would be complete without attention to this work, once the most popular book in the United States next to the Bible. It is hardly overstating the case to say that the distance from traditional views and formulations in the late twentieth century can be measured by the complete obscurity and eclipse of this one-time classic. Weber found Bunyan tasteless, but at least he recognized this work as central. The key to Bunyan's abrupt decline is in his full title: *The Pilgrim's Progress from This World to That Which is to Come.* Life is a journey, but it is a journey in which the motto is definitely not "enjoy the ride"; nor is "getting there half the fun."

Christian, the pilgrim, begins his trip because he wants to get rid of the burden on his back, and because Evangelist tells him that his hometown will be destroyed. He cannot persuade his family to come with him, and he flees their cries by covering his ears and shouting "Eternal life!" as he runs off. He meets various companions, mostly unhelpful, and suffers a wide range of dangers even before he enters by the gate and begins the life of faith. Although his burden slides away when he comes to the cross and to Christ's tomb, this is by no means the most central or dramatic of the allegorical adventures. He fights monsters, is imprisoned by a giant, gets lost, and one of his companions is murdered. Occasionally he has some good times, but even as he approaches the destination the going does not get easy. At the end of the journey, he and his fellow traveller, Ignorance, must cross a river, and in this crossing Christian falls into a fright and nearly drowns. Yet he survives and lands on the other side, where he is welcomed into the Celestial City. Ignorance, however, takes a ferry across the river, but perishes as he slides into Hell, for there is a gate to Hell even on the shores of Heaven.[11]

Undoubtedly, the monsters and the lively dialogues help. This story takes place simultaneously along the lanes and villages of seventeenth-century England, in the realm of folktales, and in the inner reaches of the Protestant Christian soul. It works because the individual episodes can be appropriated as adventures and as accounts of particular spiritual experiences. The four young heroines in Louisa May Alcott's *Little Women* "played pilgrims" when children, and later face moral and emotional challenges that match the episodes of Bunyan's story. But the central allegory remains the journey through this world to a destination that lies beyond it. Nothing that happens along the way has any intrinsic meaning apart from that goal. It is true that far along the path, in the land of Beulah, Christian is given the opportunity to view the towers of the Celestial City through a telescope. Its radiance dimly perceivable from within this life, it remains at a distance. It is never "here and now," an experience of eternity within this life. This is the closest episode in the book to an experience that C.S. Lewis would describe as "joy," or that others would categorize as a "peak experience" or a "mystical experience." By today's standards of spiritual journeys, where accounts of such unusual experiences are central, the absence of such moments is striking. For Bunyan, all of that comes *then*, and the *now* is, overall, a dangerous and deceptive place. Does this shift from the then to the now correspond to the theological "eclipse of eternity" noticed by Tony Walter in his book of the same title, or to a redrawing of the Christian mapping of life's journey so as to make eternal life a present possibility? In either case, it leads us to judge Bunyan's journey as a trek through a depleted landscape.

Moreover, there is no trace in the story of a theme that appears continuously in later Protestant piety: Jesus as the hidden companion along the way, Jesus as secretly present as friend behind the countenances of other friends, Jesus carrying the travellers when their own feet give way (as in the popular parable "Footsteps," found today in devotional knickknacks and cards in Christian bookstores). Jesus is not a character or protagonist; there is no awareness of him as really here with us in this life as well as awaiting us in the next.

On the other hand, Bunyan recognized that he might have overdrawn this picture and overdone the isolation of Christian and his journey. Part II involves the adventures of Christiana, Christian's widow, who sets off with her children after his death. This journey includes less drama, seems to take much longer, and includes a multitude of companions. Mr. Stand-fast, the group's leader, assists them through the dangers. Finally, it is his time to plunge into the river. From its midst, he tells the others, waiting on the shore:

This river has been the terror of many; yea, the thoughts of it
have also often frightened me. But now methinks I stand easy.
. . . The waters are indeed to the palate bitter, and to the stom-
ach cold. Yet the thoughts of what I am going to, and of the conduct that waits for me on the other side, doth lie as a glowing
coal at my heart.[12]

He now will experience directly all that he had hoped for. His
death is triumphant, confident, guided by the certain awareness
that the consummation of his life will confirm its earthly course.
This is the preeminent Protestant model of the "good death" for
many generations of North Americans. It is a death made happy by
firm anticipation of "that which is to come" for the believer. It is
not Christ-centered, as was the *Ars Moriendi* vision, but it is unsentimental and still allows for the ambivalence of death that even
the person of faith experiences.

Between the spirituality of *The Pilgrim's Progress* and us today
lies another development that scholars agree reshaped visions of
death and afterlife. This is the elaboration of mourning and sentimental grief over the death of a beloved person, especially spouse
or child. Ariès's label "the death of the other" encompasses this
romantic sentimentalization of family, piety, and death, which
emerged in the early to middle nineteenth century.[13] These themes
displace earlier, Puritan sparseness about "the conduct that waits
for me on the other side." This makes mourning a far more intense
experience, and allows for a cult of gravesite visits, memorials,
and elaborate funeral iconography. Here the pain of dying has become the pain of mourning. Religiously, this shift has been described as "the feminization of American religion"[14] because it so
closely identifies women as guardians of the home and moral educators of children with religiousness. Barred from the public,
male world of work, which was seen as antithetical to true piety,
women could represent and convey spiritual and emotional nurtu-
rance, and a life of faith and feeling combined. Women were specialists in caretaking, and so in grief as well.

It is from this era's preoccupations with dying, death, and bereavement as emotional experiences that we might look for the an-

cestry to some of the current literature on living with loss. Paul Rosenblatt's historical study *Bitter, Bitter Tears* confirms the continuity.[15] But the other side of this preoccupation was what Ann Douglas and others have seen as the colonization of the afterlife by middle-class sentimental piety and by "family values" in a way that would have astonished Bunyan. Whom did persons dying in the Middle Ages expect to meet at the moment of death? Christ, God the Father as judge. Whom did Bunyan's pilgrims expect to meet in the Celestial City? The one whose service they had taken, their Lord and Savior whose graciousness to them was forever beyond repayment. Whom did persons dying in the mid-nineteenth century speak of meeting? Their dead family members—although of course Jesus would be there as well.

There is simply no doubt that the blessed individual dead, who dropped out of the Protestant official picture with the end of Purgatory as a doctrine, reappear in the nineteenth century as welcoming presences. The reappearance of dead family members in afterlife imagery is not surprising given the focus on intense personal relationships within an increasingly small and isolated family unit. What is astonishing to us is how absent such figures and anticipations are from earlier sources. The angels in the medieval woodcut of the *Ars Moriendi* held up a curtain to exclude the family members from the dying person and the real drama. In contrast, family reunions in Heaven became the central core around which other elements of middle-class life were projected in nineteenth-century North American popular writings. An acknowledged expert on Heaven, Elizabeth Stuart Phelps, wrote a best-selling book, *The Gates Ajar* (1868), based on the principle that anything good or pleasing in this life would also be found on the other side. While official orthodox Christian thinkers bewailed the trivialization of last things in this consolation literature, Phelps' Heaven was filled with everything—human relationships, nice scenery, pianos—except work. It resembled a Florida retirement community, minus ill health and mortality. While it is easy to poke fun at the exploitation of religious imagery that mingles sentiment and materialism, *The Gates Ajar* was intended as consolation, to comfort those who had lost loved ones. The official teachings were thought to be too cold, too vague, too remote from what nineteenth-century persons really cared about and hoped for in their spiritual lives. We will return to this tradition and its contemporary legacies in chapter 6.

From this intense and intensely publicized preoccupation of the mid-nineteenth century with the beloved recently dead, it is indeed astonishing to find it quickly displaced in both religious thought and popular practice. Religious thinkers early in the twentieth century became more aware of issues of history and society, especially the large-scale crisis of meaning affecting European industrial culture. In responding to secularism and to the social problems of war, economic injustice, and meaninglessness, Protestant theologies shifted away from individual death and "the life everlasting" and invested in other agendas. Walter Rauschenbusch, in *A Theology for the Social Gospel* (1918), adds as an afterthought a chapter on the afterlife, in which the best he can come up with is that persons deprived of a chance for education in this life might complete degrees in Heaven.[16] By then, Christianity in its theological direction was already focusing on issues that make preoccupation with individual death appear small-minded and self-centered.

In the contemporary scene, Christian faith and practice confront the emergent secular psychotherapies, which offer alternative schemas for organizing interior life. The pastoral counseling movement is one of the most successful developments in twentieth-century North American Protestantism. Loosely defined, it focuses on counseling the living in their real, this-worldly struggles with emotional difficulties, stressful personal relationships, and, much less frequently, with the distinctively "religious" struggles of individual believers. Protestant denominations thus encouraged pastors' turning away from deathbed scenes, and supported an integration of secular psychotherapeutic theory and technique with models of "pastoral" vocation and care. Because secular psychotherapies rarely addressed issues of death and bereavement at the time of the pastoral counseling movement's establishment, the "integration" achieved did not touch on these issues either. It is not fair to say that Christians were doing nothing about dying and death, but that the new centers of energy and activity concerned other areas and issues of life. Christian pastors continued to visit the sick, preach at funerals, and comfort mourners. But these activities may have become less and less connected to other emphases within the church, just as dying and death vanished from public view in American culture at large. Hence the contrast between traditional and contemporary views of death comes so easily. We do not see the liveliness of mid-twentieth century Protestantism in its innovative model of pastoral care, but perceive a kind of backwater into which all references to death had become stagnated.

When we look back at the main motifs and images generated by the traditional writings of Christians in regard to dying and death, several points need to be reemphasized. Death and resurrection are indeed central New Testament topics, and have been bequeathed to all subsequent eras and cultural expressions of Christian faith. It is also part of Christian heritage to think in terms of a "core" of the gospel, a central narrative of salvation offered through the death and resurrection of Jesus Christ. From a historian's postmodern perspective, such a core is a myth, essentializing and fixing a fluid, endless diversity of patterns. But even acknowledging the empirical pluralism of Christian forms, the participants in these did accept that Jesus' death and resurrection mattered, mattered ultimately, and mattered so centrally that other topics and images for death could never fully replace these. In the same fashion, Jesus' death as an atonement for sin, and salvation as salvation from sin, links death and sin together for Christians. This connection is just there, although the specific theologies of atonement vary. Hence it is not just one phrase used by Paul in Romans 5:12 ("death came to all men, because all sinned") but the basic narrative framework of the passion in the four gospels that insists on such a link. Death and sin go together, and in Jesus' death is a remedy that overcomes both.

In Western Christianity at least since Augustine, this has been interpreted in a way that emphasizes guilt, penalty, models of "payment" for sin, and sin as a moral rather than ontological category. We have seen how one expression of this was the need to complexify the understandings of justice and the afterlife, but it took a long while before this occurred. A slightly different aspect of this was that Jesus as a human figure becomes a moral model, and yet retains all his power and stature as cosmic savior from sin and death. Jesus had always been cosmic savior—for Paul, for the Gospel of John, for the entire ancient church. It was his humanity that had been eclipsed, not in the official doctrine at the level of the creeds, but in the piety and iconography of the ancient world, east and west. With an intensification of interest in individual moral existence and experience, eventually Jesus as role model emerges, or perhaps reemerges, since in the Synoptic Gospels that might be precisely what is going on as he interacts with friends, followers, and strangers. By the time of the *Ars Moriendi,* the switchover is in full swing. Jesus is both comforting savior and the one whose own dying provides the ideal for each dying person to emulate.

What happens to Jesus in the Reformation? To some extent, he is brought nearer, since the whole sacred universe of saints, including the Madonna, are excluded from devotional piety. But Christ also becomes the Word and the Mediator, so much so as to some extent be stripped of his humanity again. He is too divine to become a protagonist in Bunyan's story. He is not a companion along the pilgrims' way, and the role model function is taken over by the Christian pastor (Mr. Stand-fast). Never is Jesus' connection to us as the one who redeems from sin forgotten; it is at the sepulchre that Christian's burden falls away. But Jesus is no longer there to show us how to die, how to swim across the river at the end of the journey. Perhaps this is why the earlier art of dying literature continued to be in such demand long after the Reformation. It filled a niche that some of the most formal theological systems had left vacant, and restored to Jesus the Christ a full and complete role as mediator and savior from sin and death. Nevertheless, in the phase of Protestantism that gave rise to Pietism and to Wesleyan Methodism, Jesus is once again dramatically present as welcoming presence, as the one who stands on the threshold of death. The change in the nineteenth century is that he shares this role with the recently dead or the relatives of the dying.

The story, then, is more complicated than a quantitative one-dimensional decline in religious faith or belief in an afterlife. Which role for Christ is most significant, as the one who works atonement through his death, or the ideal human who can show us how to die? Must we make a choice, or is it most desirable to affirm and explore both aspects of his being? The other element in the tradition is, most certainly, a fascination with the afterlife that ebbs and flows, sometimes fixing on justice and penalties, and sometimes on consolation. If life is a pilgrimage toward something beyond itself, if eternity is best represented as "after," then Christians have included it as part of the landscape of faith from the beginning. Resurrection is as much a part of this total landscape as is death, and the pairing of the two terms in the New Testament sets the pattern for what the ancient churches did with immortality.

Are these traditional emphases somehow wrong, misdirecting us away from "natural death" and away from this life in favor of an otherworldly eternity? A variety of theological revisionings in the twentieth century do begin from a deep sense of wrongness about the tradition. Eschatology is no longer "last things, " but an ultimate yet historical dimension to human existence. Frequently attempts to sever "resurrection" (Hebraic) from "the immortality of the soul" (Platonic) also tried to redefine this life and this world as essentially good, no longer a pale shadow of a more real, transcendent reality.

Typical of these efforts to redefine the tradition is the well-known essay by Oscar Cullman, "Immortality of the Soul or Resurrection of the Dead?" Here the author claims that an "authentic" Christian approach to death was one of horror, rejection, and combat. "This is not 'death as a friend.' This is death in all its frightful horror. This is really *the last enemy* of God."[17] Death is an enemy of God, and never a smooth transition to a "higher" or "better" place. Cullman's attack on traditional understandings was an effort to rid Christianity of what he saw as a legacy of wishful thinking, Platonic contempt for the body, and denial of death.[18] Part of the popularity of this approach was its way of declaring the tradition wrong in the name of a more "biblical" perspective. For a while and for some, this theological strategy may have some merit. But it fails at a deeper level. Not only is it an inaccurate historical approach, since there is a continuity between the New Testament, with its focus on death as linked to sin and salvation as eternal life, and what came later as far as these central doctrines go. But even as an attempt to recast the tradition so as to affirm some of the sensibilities of modern persons frustrated with Platonism and denial, it left some of the deepest messages of the gospel and the spiritual needs of contemporary believers obscured. Indeed, the very exclusion of traditional death-as-transition language, whether Platonic or not, now more clearly appears to be an expression of Christianity's partial captivity by secular perspectives that marginalize and deny death altogether. It was as a reaction to these secular sources, and not from Christian theologies, that the current renewal of concern with death traces its roots and its agendas.

The survey I have tried to relate in this chapter reveals where the tradition may make contemporary Christians uncomfortable, unable to view such texts and doctrines and practices as resources for their own faith, and their own dying and grief. An exaggerated contrast between this tradition and contemporary beliefs may miss a lot, but it does suggest why there is such a felt discrepancy between the faith of the past and the unsteadiness and confusion of the present. We may blend a diversity of pasts into one harmonious consistent image, but no matter which image we dwell on, it will bring us back to how distant that imagery appears. Such an image answers questions no one asks today, while our most urgent questions seem never to have been addressed. Even when we imagine that dying is a situation all persons everywhere in every age have had to face, there is no universal and natural way to grasp it; historical context and worldview clearly intervene. We may retrieve the past, reinterpret it, and recycle it for our current dilemmas and needs, but we know that this is what we are doing. We no longer inhabit the same space as Bunyan, or the *Ars Moriendi* authors.

In this book, I am not going to avoid that difference. But I will take up the challenge implicit in English sociologist Tony Walter's metaphor of "eclipse."[19] What is now hidden is what used to be clear. But what may now be seen, albeit dimly, is what the past's clarity and direct light obscured. The very absence of certain past motifs lets in the possibility of others. This is how a tradition is remapped, this is how a landscape of faith is revisioned. And this is why, in the "Meditations" between the chapters of this book, we find in the passion narrative new dimensions, new voices, and fresh possibilities for the spirit, that in the traditional Christian readings and appropriations were mute or overwhelmed by other, dominant motifs. In the tradition, even in those places where Christ's function as role model for the dying was prominent, there appears what to us now seems a squeamishness about the fullness of his humanity; not of his embodiment or of his mortality, but of his full humanity as an emotional being. It is part of the eclipse of much of the tradition that certain key scenes and images appear much brighter than before. Gethsemane is one of these.

MEDITATION 1: GETHSEMANE
Mark 14:32–42; Matthew 26:36–46; Luke 22:39–46

Here is a scene with no human witnesses. Jesus is alone in the garden on the night before his death. Not only is this one of the few places where Jesus is alone, but here we are allowed to see and hear his innermost feelings. "Deeply distressed and troubled"; "overwhelmed with sorrow to the point of death"; "being in anguish": the emotion words are stark and extreme. Jesus feels, feels deeply and terribly. He does not want what he know lies ahead: death. Although his final affirmation remains, "Not my will but yours be done," the struggle against his own feelings, fears, and desire to avoid what will come very soon is a cruel one. Today this struggle is a point of contact for our postdenial perspective, to take his feelings and feel them as our own. Indeed, it is this scene that opens us to the whole passion narrative, in a manner few previous ages could have understood or dwelt upon.

What makes Jesus weep and beg God for a last-minute change of plan here? Is it the horror of death? Is death God's enemy, and does Jesus weep because he is about to be conquered by that enemy? This is modern language, not given in the story. But it is clear that Jesus in the story weeps for himself, is anguished and distressed for himself. He does not weep for *others'* sins, and he has none of his own to weep for. This is where the authors of *Ars Moriendi* ran against the texts' own wording. The theological meaning of Jesus' death as punishment and payment for sin so controlled their thinking that when they spoke of Jesus' weeping, they could only relate it back to *our* repentance. Neither they nor we can actually claim that this motif belongs to Jesus directly. But their reason is a focus on the link between death and penance, while ours is a contemporary preoccupation and empathy with the emotional anguish so clearly evident in the story. Whatever Jesus is doing in Gethsemane and later on the cross, he is not repenting. Sin does not apply to him, as it does to all the rest of us. The traditional motif misleads here.

Yet we see and feel here, as did the medieval authors, that Jesus does not let passionate grief separate him from God, and does not let his divinity separate him from passionate grief. Instead of rising above passions and sorrows into a realm of pure contemplation, Jesus sinks down into anguish and sorrow, anxiety and depression. He refuses to deny pain and sorrow, and it is in this refusal that we too may join him, watching although his first disciples slept. Jesus refuses denial, refuses the road of joyful dying or even of stoic resignation. He does not keep a stiff upper lip with his Father, nor does he pretend not to truly feel.

This scene subverts dualistic, Platonic views of the person not because resurrection and immortality are in themselves so different, but because Jesus as whole embodied person is so fully engaged in his prayer for a reprieve. The bloody sweat on his forehead is a testimony to this. Nor is there any sense that what is about to happen will happen only to his body, that his soul will remain unscathed. Death will engulf the whole person, and it is as a whole person that Jesus resists it here. Just as it is impossible to sever soul from body, so efforts to decide which nature—his human or his divine—truly suffered, fail to accept the fullness of the experience.

When we meet Jesus in his pain, we too may resist the urge to deny, to pretty up, to hastily subvert our pain by claims that "It is all for the best." Unwilling to face the full consequences of the Incarnation, some early Christians turned away from any vision of God as suffering, as truly vulnerable to pain and death. When we watch with Jesus in Gethsemane, we resist our contemporary edition of this heresy, we put aside our culture's silence and denial of death. We put it aside without reliance upon a nostalgic caricature of good death or a romantic representation of dying as a family reunion. We cannot say that death is good in itself when God himself weeps in its face. Jesus is "overwhelmed with sorrow to the point of death" because he knows he will soon be at this point, and is anticipating his end.

His end, but not his defeat. There is no military imagery here. Death is not personified as the enemy, and Satan the tempter does not appear, even indirectly, in this scene. It is wrong to import this language, wrong to invoke heroic defiance or conquest metaphors for how Jesus faces death. When this is done, as in Cullman's essay, it is really importing twentieth-century scientific fantasies of control and defeat of death. Horror and terror may be there, but Jesus does not encounter an enemy, an externalized other, only his own desire, acknowledged as fully his own, to "let this cup pass from me."

There have been countless ways to sleep, to avoid the task of watching with Jesus in the garden. We may now experience the invitation to do so in a new way, freer to sink down with him into an encounter with impending death that permits sorrow and anguish, and finds these even in the heart of the Son of God.

"Death Is Natural"

I.

In this chapter I will describe and discuss the foundational imagery used by the newer death and dying literature. Although this body of writings contains many variations, and includes discussions of a wide range of contemporary issues, I will try to grasp its unity, its shared assumptions and images. A "death awareness movement," a broad-based advocacy of certain ideas and practices, is an accurate way to characterize the sources and grassroots popularity of the themes we will examine. This movement's most central claim is that "death is natural," and "death is a part of life," and therefore that death, like birth, *belongs* in our picture of human beings. This claim is what we must examine, carefully and reflectively. What is actually meant by it? How is it understood and used today? What is *not* intended by those who use it, although much might logically follow from it? How has this claim about death's naturalness come to be seen as an important, novel, challenging stance in contemporary North American society?

Let's begin by clarifying what the death awareness movement is. The first contemporary writings on dying and death are in the anthology by Herman Feifel, *The Meaning of Death,* published in 1959.[1] There is no doubt that this set some precedents for the

movement that followed. Even the earliest volume was interdisciplinary, willing to look at death squarely as a psychological and
social problem, and anxious to include discussions of it within
contemporary social scientific frameworks that seemed to be otherwise silent about it. Overall, there was an existentialist influence
on this project, but not a highly technical philosophic emphasis.
When Elisabeth Kübler-Ross's *On Death and Dying* hit the market in 1969, and became very successful as a gateway to wider
public awareness of dying and death, the relatively narrow reader-
ship and research tone of earlier volumes and theorists gave way
to a more general audience, a more accessible mode of communication, a message much more easily packaged and transmitted. In
the wake of the movement, earlier works, such as *Counseling the
Dying* by Margaretta Bowers and associates, were reissued.[2] After
Kübler-Ross, workshops for the public on topics related to dying,
grief, and death became common, and even at events designed for
professionals and specialists there has been room—although much
less room than twenty-five years ago—for those whose interest is
personal rather than professional.

The introduction of hospice from Britain into this country in
1967 coincided with this burst of public interest in dying and
death. Hospice is an institution, an organization, as well as a philosophy; it began as an alternative to ordinary medical care for the
terminally ill. As I will show in the next chapter, hospice addresses
the problems that arise within the hospital setting, problems
Kübler-Ross and others vividly portrayed. Early death awareness
writings and workshops paved the way for hospice's acceptance in
this country. Yet hospice is not identical with the death awareness
movement, for the latter includes a variety of institutions and
methods of communication and advocacy.

In this study, I will focus primarily on the ideas advanced and
widely embraced. Nevertheless, readers should be aware that
events such as weekend workshops for cancer patients, public tele-
vision interviews and documentaries on topics of dying, scholarly
groups such as ADEC (Association for Death Education and
Counseling) and large conferences held at study centers (e.g.,

King's College Centre in London, Ontario) are all ways that make the newer death and dying language accessible and available to a wide range of persons. In addition, tapes and books, such as autobiographical tales of the author's own struggles with terminal illness, are available. Specialized support groups have even developed for the sick and the bereaved. For the local church, a fine work such as Paul Irion's *Hospice and Ministry* systematically tries to bring the ideas and practices of hospice into the sphere of church and pastoral care so that pastors may involve themselves with the work of hospice teams and promote the values of hospice among their congregations. Meanwhile, schools, funeral homes, and even veterinary clinics have become participants in the counseling of the bereaved, and spread perspectives and imageries of the death awareness movement.

A movement in this loose sense is not a cult, a small tight-knit group of fanatical true believers, out to change the world or flee from it. Members of cult groups may be mobilized for making converts, for intensive fund-raising, or even for group suicide. But the presence of a few cult-like groups on the outskirts of the death awareness movement should only serve to dramatize how different this new language for dying and death has been. There is no geographical center for it, no tightly structured hierarchy of individuals running a mini-world of their own. It is a serious mistake to criticize the death awareness movement as if it were a kind of conspiracy, closely orchestrated by a small number of devious individuals intent on controlling the rest of us. Moreover, the social critique of contemporary America offered in the death awareness movement is unlike that of any radical outsider group; it is not intended as a call to abandon middle-class life, private property, ordinary expectations about family, education, politics, or God. The stereotyped image of a cult may be itself inaccurate even to describe the groups usually labelled as such, but it is very important to recognize how unlike this the principal organizations and activities of the death awareness movement are. Its ideas and images have been widely adopted in American society because they make sense, they feel right, they fit with how many people see things.

I have heard, moreover, another criticism of the movement: it is increasingly dominated by professionals. Such professionalization over the last few decades makes it all the more mainstream and unlike a cult. Conferences and workshops, for instance, routinely offer continuing education credits for those seeking credentials as counselors. Does this professionalization represent another kind of conspiracy, one of counselors and social workers to manage universal, simple human experiences that people ought to cope with on their own? This worry echoes earlier accusations that therapists create the need for their services, by turning ordinary problems into "illness" for which specialized help is required. Unfortunately, there is massive evidence that dying and bereavement in our society are not simple matters that people intuitively know how to handle. This kind of conspiracy theory falters, like so many before it, whenever those who use it start by assuming that the problems with which therapists cope are in some sense manufactured and therefore unreal. Indeed, there are now professionals for bereavement counseling and for a variety of specialized services for the dying and their families, but the death awareness movement is no figment of therapists' greed for clients and power. The problems have been with us all along. In fact, the death awareness movement is probably appealing because it can say *something,* and bring a framework of meaning to experiences that need attention.

Rather than a conspiracy, the death awareness movement is an advocacy movement, with an explicit agenda. Its ideas may be new, challenging, unsettling, and different from the ways we in North America are used to thinking about things. Advocates of these ideas often feel that they go against the status quo, and that a movement to implement these ideas is justified. There is an agenda: they hope to make contemporary persons see death as natural. They want to help those who wish to die "naturally" do so. They want our society to return death to its rightful place as a natural part of life, back from its current exile. One may appropriately ask, "What does it mean to claim that 'death is natural'?" Particular individuals and groups say this, feel they must continue to say it, and believe they must organize and advocate for such a stance.

Even if others acknowledge what they say feels right, and makes sense, proponents still insist that their message has not truly been heard, and needs to be reiterated. This paradox is part of the situation I will explore.

II.

> *Death is natural; it is a part of life.*
> *We should accept death as a natural part of life.*
> *Like birth, death is a natural event.*

Statements such as these by now sound familiar. They are mantras, repeated throughout the newer literature of dying and death. Since they do not provide new information, what do those who repeat them tell us? What is really being affirmed, and what excluded? We can say easily enough that these are statements about death in general, and not about particular modes of death. Here there is no room for the contrast between "natural" deaths and homicides, suicides, and accidental deaths. That categorization, although legally relevant, is not truly part of the newer language at all. No more is the classic religious distinction of "natural" versus "supernatural," which stands utterly outside the vision of the contemporary movement. Instead, "death is natural" serves as a philosophical claim, a claim that those who assert it believe needs special, insistent affirmation today. Why? Often the best way to illuminate what a general claim means is to ask what it argues against.

The opposite of "death is natural" is "death is unnatural; it is not a part of life; it does not belong; it should not happen." It is just this stance against which those in the death awareness movement mobilize. In their eyes American society has believed in death-free existence, has constructed an illusory image of life without death, of persons who do not grow old and never die. This is the voice of denial, which most of us have grown up with and have internalized. Therefore, all our serious thinking about death is put off until the indefinite future of someday (the revealing title of a book by Andrew Malcolm on his mother's death). When death happens, it is violent and on TV, and therefore unreal and griefless, or it is violent and "unnatural" and therefore must be someone's fault. For the most part, people assume that death does not belong; it is invisible, something that will never happen to them. It has been exiled to specialized institutional settings, and specialized experts are paid to cope with it, rather than ordinary people themselves.

To insist that death is natural today means to challenge this perspective. In the next chapter we will look at the specific environment, the contemporary hospital, where the battle over death's presence and the attempt to exile death become particularly vivid. But in this initial discussion, we may say that the primary imagery and theme of the death awareness movement is to insist that death *belongs,* it is a predictable and universal ending to all human lives. To repress or deny it brings far more grief than to acknowledge it. People who wish to be free of death do not really escape from pain and fear; they actually magnify these through avoiding reality. Death denied is more fearful, more powerful and destructive, than death as "natural." In its own more directly psychological language, the death awareness movement agrees with Ariès' claim: "It is not that death was originally wild, and became tame; it is we who have made it wild." By forgetting or denying that death is natural, we have made it worse.

A sign of how central this message is, are the frequent references in contemporary death and dying literature to Tolstoy's story, "The Death of Ivan Ilych." It is far from the only major work of modern literature dealing with mortal illness, but appears to have made more of an impact than any others. This tale of the miserable lonely death of an upper-middle-class Everyman was written in 1886 and predates intensive care units, ventilators, DNRs, and the environment of high-tech hospitals. Yet the story seems to speak to contemporary North Americans, perhaps even more than it did to late nineteenth-century Russians. "Ivan Ilych's life had been most simple, most ordinary and therefore most terrible," the author tells us early on.[3] Why? Ivan lived an upper-middle-class existence; he was what we might call a yuppified careerist, in a loveless marriage to a woman as selfish as he. Indeed, Ivan had lived in ignorance of life, death, God, and self, not unlike his family and entire social class.

The story begins as his colleagues at work learn of his death, briefly consider who will fill his vacant position, and comfortably reflect on how "It is he who is dead and not I." Ivan too must discard this attitude if he is to come into a truthful relation with himself and his death. The main part of the tale is told from Ivan's perspective: as he injures himself by a fall from a stepladder, becomes aware of a pain in his side, and gradually slips into mortal illness. He encounters doctors who treat him as impersonally and deceitfully as he has treated clients in his work. He is completely alienated from his family members, who consider his illness an affront to their happiness. The only person who cares for him is Gerasim, a young servant, who is also the only one in the story who accepts that death will happen *to him* one day, and thus can accept Ivan's dying as a natural part of life.

When Ivan's initial conviction that "death happens to someone else" starts to break down in the face of his own mortal illness, death appears as "It," a dreaded faceless presence. "It" haunts and terrorizes him, reducing his life to ashes and laying bare the emptiness of his soul.[4] This "It" is an externalized enemy, the only way death can be known by those who have carried with them a false portrait of a deathless human being. In Ivan's hopeless struggle against "It," we see a fantasy of a malevolent external presence as a horrible prelude to a more conscious and complete acknowledgement of his own death. Eventually, Ivan grows into such an acceptance, but only by jettisoning his entire past; he recognizes his life as empty and meaningless, although he had followed all the rules. He admits to himself that what he had considered a good life was in reality "a terrible and huge deception which had hidden both life and death."[5]

Tolstoy's story appears contemporary, and fits so beautifully within the framework of contemporary death and dying literature, in spite of its author's distance from hospitals, medical technology, and the whole medicalized situation of the dying today. Why? Perhaps because Ivan is not worried about Hell and damnation, or indeed any kind of after-death existence. His problem is with himself, his dying, his lack of authentic relationship to both. His major problem, next to fear of "It," is the utter loneliness and isolation of his struggle. Everyone around him pretends, first that he will recover, and then that what is happening to him will not touch them, will not interfere with their lives and pleasures. In a world where death does not belong and is "unnatural," the dying people are excluded and silenced. No communication, even at the end of the story, occurs between the dying Ivan and those around him, nor is God an active presence and participant in his struggle. Whatever Christian imagery appears in the story, especially at the end, God is never there as personal consoler, as welcoming presence, as companion in death. Ivan's lack of religious faith is not, however, what contemporary authors who cite this story notice. Although Tolstoy might have found this the ultimate source of Ivan's problems, clearly Ivan's denial of death's "natural" presence and his exaggerated terror and isolation are what make this story gripping today.

If we count as "the past" anything written prior to Freud—as is common in psychological literature—then "The Death of Ivan Ilych" is virtually the only text from the past that has a firm and distinguished place in the present discussions of death and dying. Even Freud, whose essay "On Mourning and Melancholia" is often cited, may not be so contemporary. Freud's work is mentioned at the start of literature surveys on the psychology of mourning, but not as a voice who speaks directly to us today. Regardless of the date of the story, Ivan Ilych dies *now,* and his issues are our issues. If people wish to see what "death is natural" means now, in this cultural context, this story helps us situate the claim. The choice is set forth: accept death as a part of life, or die struggling as Ivan did against pervasive interior and social denial of death. To say that death is natural is not to claim it has no spiritual meaning, nor is it to say it is good, wonderful, glorious, or beautiful. It is, however, to claim that death ought to be accepted as an intrinsic part of life's totality. Tolstoy, so it seems, says this more clearly and eloquently than anyone else.

III.

Does Ivan's denial of death result from a universal human fear or is it specific to his social class and culture? Is it hard for all human beings to maintain that death is natural, or is this a truth once known that people have forgotten? Gerasim the peasant servant exemplifies the alternative, authentic attitude toward death. Gerasim accepts the natural fact that all persons die. His kindness toward Ivan and his acceptance of Ivan's impending death, stem from an outlook that treats death as a part of life, in contrast to all the upper-middle-class persons in the story. From Tolstoy's point of view, peasant values include this realism, this deep accomodation to life's basic limits. Middle-class life is a sustained deception, a flight from these. To use the terms from Ariès introduced earlier, Gerasim represents the "tame death" that some people in the past, and some simpler societies even today, accept as a given. But modern Americans, the Ivan Ilychs of the world, have made death "wild." By extension, attitudes like those of Ivan Ilych have built the high-tech medicine that perpetuates our own denial of death.

This contrast within Tolstoy's story haunts enough of the contemporary literature that one may speak of widespread nostalgia for tame death as one dimension of the call to remember that death is natural. It is not, then, that psychologists and thanatologists have discovered that death is natural; they are attempting to *rediscover* this truth. How does this nostalgia work? Kübler-Ross evokes it early in *On Death and Dying,* and other authors repeat this strategy.[6] Once, not so long ago (or, in a culture other than ours), people lacked hospitals, but nevertheless had a sense of peace and control over their own deaths. They could count on others being there for them, and could expect to die in a familiar setting. They could anticipate their own death through the body's hidden cues. "When he knew that his time was near . . . " goes the traditional phrasing. (This knowledge is possible only when the terminally ill person is not stupified by pain medication or terrified by its absence.) In this kind of tame death as we have seen, death is a community event; there is no isolation of the dying from neighbors or children. Exposure to death occurs as a normal part of growing up. Not only is the dying never abandoned, but others learn how to accept and care for a dying person. The role of the doctor is not exaggerated; if present at all he is present as comforter, not as a representative of science, nor is he a warrior about to lose a battle against death. We the readers can relate to this, lulled into forgetting that the past was never that simple. Had Kübler-Ross written about the village death of small children or of a woman in childbirth, the spell of such scenes over us might be much harder to maintain.

In this vision of death, it does not matter if disease or accident is the actual cause. What matters is that death comes within the normal range of experience, and the dying person dies in his or her ordinary home environment. Even if there is not much preparation time, the death is not anomalous, shocking, disruptive of people's worldview. No one is terrified by its approach. It is not casual or brutal, but by comparison with deaths in our own society, it is rather routine. This is exactly the kind of death Gerasim expects to die. This is why, although he had cheerfully and willingly cared for Ivan, he does it not out of deep personal devotion, but from a taken-for-granted sense that this is his duty. Someone will, he knows, have to do the same for him someday.[7]

If Gerasim saw his caretaking as part of his duty to his master, others who intentionally invoke the tame death model as a contrast to the present have noted how care for the dying became a religious duty even extending beyond the family and others in the community. The late twentieth-century hospice movement presents its aims by recalling the specialized care once provided by religious orders to the dying. Hospices in the Middle Ages were places where pilgrims, strangers, travellers, and other displaced sick persons were welcomed. It was the obligation of religious orders to run them, to offer a tame death even for those separated from permanent communities. Because travel was hazardous, and dying on pilgrimage was not unusual, such provisions were necessary. At a practical level, this solved the problem of whose responsibility it was to bury indigent strangers. The ideal of caring for strangers as a substitute for ordinary care by one's own family may be part of a very long Western tradition of altruism and hospitality. It had its counterpart in Japan, where Buddhist monks cared for and buried dying pilgrims. In such settings, the medical care may have been nonexistent or atrocious by our standards, but the human concern for those about to die was manifest, and the explicit goal was to make a space where dying could happen and happen "well."

Before we procede, the oddity of this nostalgia should be identified. It is customary for religious spokespersons to voice nostalgia for the good old days, and indeed they are routinely cast for this role. It is unusual to find such widespread nostalgia among psychologists, sociologists, and others who derive their identity from social sciences. A significant dimension of that identity has, in the last hundred years or more, been its distance from religion, from "tradition," and its endorsement of newer, more secular patterns of life.[8] Psychologists are expected to sever themselves from nostalgia, to address life today as liberated from traditional restrictions, as filled with possibilities that the past prohibited. On almost all other topics, this has indeed been their stance. Any issues connected with sexuality, to take the most obvious example, will follow this pattern. One will never find a drop of nostalgia for the good old days when sexual repression was the norm, when "people didn't talk about such things," in any writings by psychologists or those influenced by them. So to the degree that any nostalgia for death the old-fashioned way is voiced at all in such quarters, it is an anomaly, a break with what has come to be the expected self-identity of psychological thinkers

Now, however, we must balance this nostalgia theme with another perspective, more familiar to psychological and particularly psychoanalytic theory. According to this view, all humans everywhere have feared and denied death. All humans everywhere share an unconscious that does not allow for death. In our unconscious, death is impossible and unreal. Thus, the struggle against denial of death must be a struggle against universal, powerful forces within the self, and not just cultural representations. The variations in how different cultures and historical eras cope with death are, from this point of view, much less significant than Ariès and others who depend upon nostalgia for tame death make them out to be. We are all, each and every one of us, death-deniers. This approach draws upon both psychological universalism and existentialism for its power. Psychological language in and of its very nature assumes universal forces and structures. Drives, defense mechanisms, and so forth are assumed to operate in all persons in fundamentally similar ways. Although there is room for cultural diversity in terms of how these are expressed, that all persons everywhere share basic psychological patterns is a given of this discourse. To state this simply, from the viewpoint of psychological theory, one may ask if Freud and earlier nineteenth-century thinkers "discovered" the unconscious (as in Ellenberger's *The Discovery of the Unconscious*), but it is not a possible psychological question to ask if anyone before the modern period had an unconscious in the first place. They did, they must have, if they are to be counted as truly human.

How then do those who prefer this language, this postulated unity of the human race as over against its diverse cultural manifestations, account for the very different perspectives on death that Ariès and the nostalgia advocates stress? First, they claim that denial as a basic psychological mechanism takes a wide variety of forms. To assume that death is a transition to an afterlife or to a new incarnation in the cycle of *samsara* would be a more elaborate denial of death than believing, "Death cannot be real for me," but it amounts to the same thing psychologically. In both cases, death's finality and reality are denied, whether in religious visions of something beyond death or in contemporary society's silence and avoidance. We have merely exchanged one form of denial for another. Such an argument, however, extends a kind of secular rationality endemic to most psychological thought, by reducing incredibly diverse cultural practices down to a few defense mechanisms.

The second strategy is to de-nostalgize the past by paying special attention to beliefs and practices that show how fearful and complicated death used to be. For instance, in many of Freud's writings one finds descriptions about fear of the dead, malevolent ghosts, and rituals to banish the newly dead from the realm of the living.[9] The purpose in citing these is to prove that death was never easily accepted as natural; it always disconcerted and disrupted, and it always provoked a great deal of hidden ambivalence. Anger, guilt, and fear accompanied death even in contexts where today's denials would have been unthinkable. If by "natural" one means "simple" and "acceptable," then it is just wrong to claim that death was ever this way in the minds of peoples of the past. Freudians do not, of course, believe in malevolent ghosts, in the anger of the dead against the living, or any of these beliefs themselves. What they believe is that death is always a source of anxiety and fear, which in the past could be projected in any number of fantastic ways. It is we—more rational and psychologically oriented than our ancestors—who must try to cope with death's terror minus supernatural overbeliefs. No wonder we feel death to be horrifying and unbearable; we have lost the option of projecting its natural terror away from ourselves. Ernest Becker's *The Denial of Death* spells out this argument in great depth and detail.[10] It counteracts nostalgia by trying to paint the past as death-denying and superstitious, while we are rational, secular—and still terrified of death.

The contemporary death and dying literature has not bought this argument, however, and it continues to draw upon nostalgic scenes of "natural" death in contrast to today's alternative. The strict Freudian argument that all accomodations with death are illusion is rarely if ever heard, and practices relating to angry ghosts are seldom cited as relevant to how people in the past died and mourned. The contemporary death and dying literature has not entirely turned its back on Freud and psychoanalysis, nor has it abandoned psychological universalism as its primary vocabulary. But the validity of "death is natural" is so overwhelming, and the negative example of Ivan Ilych so close at hand, that it is not surprising how Freudian perspectives drop out or are themselves reinterpreted. For example, some would hold that the Freudian claim, "We can never believe in our own death," is itself an example of contemporary denial.[11]

It would be admirable if this rejection of the thesis that all people everywhere have always feared and denied death, as represented by

Becker, were due to growing appreciation of cultural diversity, and with it a suspicion about psychological language itself. I do not believe that this is the case. Interest in cultural diversity has not been a strong feature of the death awareness movement, as its pervasive "we" language, meant to cover all of American society regardless of race, ethnicity, religion, and national origin, might indicate. I have faithfully repeated this language, and there is some justification for maintaining it. The basic theories endorsed and developed by death awareness movement advocates continue to be cast in language that is universalistic in this sense. Moreover, the nostalgic scenes cited by advocates of natural death do not reveal much interest in the varieties of past practice; in the differences between traditional natural death in the colonial United States and in Japan, for example. Such differences are as irrelevant to the use of these scenes as are the definitively Russian elements in Tolstoy. So long as the people of the past lived in small tight-knit communities and died at home (or in hospices while on pilgrimage!), they qualify as exemplars of "death as natural." What is most real about the past is its difference from the present. And once again, if we find that "death as natural" is linked to the choice between death as an intrinsic part of human life and a death-free existence, we may indeed find cultural variations insignificant. No culture of the past, and few today, have the luxury to live as Ivan Ilych tried to. Simple, ordinary, and terrible. Unnaturally.

IV.

Did medieval religious orders and pilgrims consider death as natural? Is this even a theme in Tolstoy's story? To say that death is a part of human life, unavoidable for all, is not exactly the same as the image of natural used by contemporary thinkers. What is the difference? The "naturalness" of death seems to carry connotations that go beyond universal and inevitable. Moreover, the Christian element in both Tolstoy and medieval hospices does not focus at all on death as natural, but nevertheless maintains that death comes to all, is inescapable, and cannot be successfully blocked out. Thus, it is not a clear and exclusive choice to use "natural" as the opposite of "denied." What exactly does it mean to say that anything is natural? If something is natural does that say it is fundamentally good or beneficial? That it ought to happen? That it is fruitless and undignified to complain about it or try to change it? It is time to explore what connotations, obvious and hidden, go along with "nature" and "natural" as used today. Here we enter territory that is explicitly philosophical, mythical, theological, even if most of the death awareness movement has not been philosophically trained, nor used to interpreting the hidden religious assumptions behind psychological claims.

The most plausible initial association, one that perhaps all contemporary thinkers simply assume, is that "death is natural" means that it is a biological fact. Human beings are living organisms and so follow the laws of all organisms; we die just like trees, crows, and cows do. As "natural" in this sense, we can be studied as living organisms by biologists. The problem with this is that it is precisely this natural scientific perspective, when exemplified in medicine, that the death awareness movement finds overwhelmingly objectionable and inadequate. Human beings, including and especially hospital patients, are not simply organisms. We are thinking, feeling, reflecting, and experiencing persons. Our deaths may be biologically identical to the deaths of crows and cows, but we know that this says very little about death in human experience. The very triumph of this naturalist perspective, the reduction of human to living organism, is what has helped create the problems for which the death awareness movement proposes answers. Yes, death is a biological fact, but when advocates for natural death repeat, "Death is a natural fact of life," this is definitely *not* what they want to reinforce.

But what about study of death as a part of the human sciences? Isn't this tied to the claim that death is natural? After all, before the contemporary flowering of death and dying research, death as a human experience was dealt with either medically, or was managed by religions. The latter held prior rights to it, so to speak, and gave the impression that death was therefore off-limits for scientific research. The big transition, according to this view, came when death was included as a field of secular study. Death and dying then became research topics appropriate to medicine, psychiatry, psychology, social work, education, and sociology. Using scientific method and problem solving, persons trained in these intellectual disciplines can begin to conceptualize and formulate hypotheses about dying or mourning as human experiences. The original ideal of "scientific thanatology" hoped to accomplish this. Had death and dying remained a scientific subspecialty, a branch of psychiatry, then to understand "death is natural" as "studied by those who consider themselves scientists" would have been more common than it is today.

But this is not what developed. Instead, discussion of death and dying burst the bounds of a scientific research area and became a "movement," with a language adapted to the needs of nonresearchers. Death is something all can speak of, including those in the practical professions, medical patients, and the general public. The death awareness movement is inclusive of research, but is not by any means limited to those who identify themselves as scientists or who have any interest in application of the scientific method to dying and grief. The explicit hostility of Kübler-Ross to scientific thanatology may have reflected a personal quirk, but it also suggested how ambivalence about scientific expertise is tied to the expressions of this movement. In a movement where personal experience with life-threatening illness was considered an alternative source of expertise, the limits of the scientific researcher model were apparent. A sign of how partial the scientific research ideal is and remains is that conferences on death and dying routinely divide program presentations into "research" and "experiential" styles, leaving ample room for both even in the most educationally rigorous venues. Although all of the presenters may have research credentials, they are permitted to depart from a research model in order to affectively engage their audiences at an experiential and personal level.

When this relative eclipse of science and the scientific thanatology ideals happened, other associations for "nature" came to the fore. Nature became linked not with natural science but with Mother Nature, and with a spiritual vision positing an invisible immanent harmony between individual and cosmos. These connotations of "nature" and "natural" may indeed be the keys to the death awareness movement's success. If death is a part of nature, a natural event such as birth, it is not primarily because both death and birth can be studied by science, but because Nature is a harmonious ordered system within which humans as individuals can hope to find meaning. (I deliberately capitalize the *N* because I want to stress how like a divine principle this meaning of the term seems.) In short, Nature is here a mythical motif, not a scientific concept. Those who use this motif believe that if we try to live outside of or at odds with Nature, we will come to grief. Human fulfillment can only be found in ways that are congruent with the limits of Nature; to attempt to escape or deny these is hubris and will be destructive on an individual, a social, and a global scale.

Note how Nature in this sense is fundamentally neutral if not positively benevolent. This Nature is very far from the "Nature red in tooth and claw" of Darwinism as social philosophy in the later nineteenth century, nor is it "cruel" and "hostile" as in Freud's *The Future of an Illusion*. The first expression focuses on competition and predation, the second simply assumes that Nature is an enemy needing to be subdued by our willpower. By contrast, what fascinates us now about Nature is that it is an ecological system in which deaths play a role, belong, and are appropriate. To claim, "Death is natural," is to evoke this image of a reality beyond the merely human but inclusive of it.

Those who rely on this imagery of Nature go further. Our problem in the West may have begun by hypostatizing Nature as a power against which we must fight and from which we must separate ourselves if we are to be truly, transcendently human. Here what begins as a claim about the naturalness of death extends out toward a critique of modern, Cartesian, Newtonian, Western modes of living, knowing, and being. Is our problem with death as a natural part of life due to our reluctance to consider ourselves as part of, rather than outside, Nature as a system? In this critique, we are the heirs of a disastrous attempt at separating ourselves from the world of which we are born to be a part. According to this view, the Western model of knowing divorces subject from object, mind from matter, self from world, so as to alienate all of us from our roots, from our grounding in Nature and the world. We have set up dichotomies in which God, soul, and history are all set over against body and nature. No wonder we find ourselves unable to include death in any portrait of ourselves. No wonder Nature's presence is obscured, externalized into the evil "It" of death as faced by Ivan Ilych.

Today another dichotomy sure to be mentioned as part of this critique is that while mind and God and history are all masculine, nature and body are feminine. At least in Western thinking, these terms frequently carry such connotations, sometimes as unconscious reverberations, and sometimes very directly and explicitly. In the opinion of those who voice this critique, not only does this split make the Western worldview dualistic, but unlike Taoist yin-yang philosophy, our dualism is unbalanced. We have placed what is masculine above what is feminine in our mythology. Traditionally, God and spirit are superior to nature and body, even if both sides of the duality are good and potentially harmonious. But very often, it is claimed, the Western worldview has pathologized the weaker terms of each pair. Nature and body are more suspect, less worthy, just as women are believed to be lesser beings than men. From this perspective, the task for all contemporary persons is to restore equal dignity to both or to move beyond dualisms altogether. Accordingly, the language of "death as natural" is gendered, so as to return reality and full worth to the despised feminine side of the dichotomized worldview. To claim that death is as natural as birth is, in this context, no accident; both birth and death are coded as feminine. Along with other links to nature, these express the repressed undervalued feminine realities in a world too long dominated by one-sided masculine modes of knowledge. Those who argue in this fashion often maintain that the actual natures of men and women are not at stake; it is the way Western culture has constructed gender-specific categories for our metaphysics that matters, and that must be reexamined.[12]

Even if nature is rarely explicitly labelled as "Mother Nature" in any of the death awareness movement's writings, do these meanings pervade its literature? Are they part of the subtext, the connotations of the claims about death that play so central a role in the new language? I believe so. This is not to say all who speak of "Death as natural" consciously intend or agree with these meanings. Nor do I accept the above diagnosis of the source of contemporary Western society's problems with dying and death. But what moved the death awareness movement away from scientific thanatology toward what it became, seems to have been its welcome of this cluster of gender-specific images and rejection of their dichotomized opposites. This connection to mythical Nature helped make language of "natural death" much more powerful and persuasive.

But how did this occur? What pathways of symbolic association were at work? Assuming that the above analysis of Western modes of knowledge and gendered power is not so obvious, how did it become a hidden dimension of the death awareness movement's agenda? There may be several levels of answers to these questions, but one seems striking, and fateful. Recall the dates for Kübler-Ross's first book and the introduction of hospice to this country. What else was happening for Americans in the late 1960s? The most dominant, divisive, and newsworthy event of the time was the Vietnam War. It is no coincidence that Kübler-Ross insisted that if we all took time off to think about our own deaths, there would be a chance for world peace.[13] In short, to accept death as natural implies renunciation of war, while denial of death will make us murderous toward others. (One might think that exactly the opposite would hold true: acceptance of death gives permission for war, while its denial will lead to greater reluctance to engage in death-dealing behavior.) What can we make now, decades later, of such claims? Why does it seem appropriate for Samuel Southard to characterize the early phase of the death awareness movement as participating in "the post-Vietnam ethos"?[14] How are these concerns related to gender-coding? Very directly.

War and warfare and the heroic stance of combat are traditionally understood as masculine, and imagery associated with them is going to be masculine in everyone's consciousness. The military model stresses violent death as a sacrifice, but valid only when it serves some purpose or ideal. Otherwise, to die is to be killed, to be defeated. Enthusiasm for war might have been sustained were there some widely accepted and clearly defined goal for the war; instead, it appeared in televised images of meaningless, violent death, often delivered to civilians and prisoners, unheroic and chaotic. Reporting of the war focused on stories of its brutality and public debates over its morality. Therefore, to undermine the military model and its imagery became a prevalent option among those protesting and calling for an end to the Vietnam conflict. This same model had been applied to medicine, with the doctor as the warrior who fights valiantly against disease and death, taking on the power of a heroic self-sacrificing savior. The widespread use of this imagery for medicine preceded the Vietnam War, of course; it is the first image of healing and medicine listed and discussed in William F. May's *The Physician's Covenant,* precisely because it was so well established.[15] But the coincidence of the bitterly controversial war fought by real men but for uncertain aims highlighted the moral limits of this imagery more intensely than ever before. It was at this time that the irony of the military model applied to medicine came to the fore: when the doctor was "defeated," it was the patient who died. To fight the medical battle against death does not require the doctor's life to be at stake, but that of the patient. It is the dying patient who becomes a visible reproach to the doctor's failed military strategy and who risks abandonment when the fantasy of combat victory goes wrong.

In direct contrast to warfare, birth, nursing, and caretaking are all traditionally feminine activities, and in our society have been practiced overwhelmingly by women even in settings away from home and the private "feminine" sphere. These activities become for the "death as natural" imagery valid and appropriate symbolic links to death. Thus, in the death awareness movement's language, those activities assumed to be "women's work" are given priority over activities associated with men; the symbol of "nature" carries with it a bond to women, women's tasks, and women's areas of expertise. It is not hard to document how pervasive and taken-for-granted this association is. A speaker at a recent death awareness conference gave the original meaning for "natural" as "close to birth," and hinted that women have always had easier access to wisdom in "natural matters." More crassly, others insist that when it comes to caretaking for elderly parents, "Don't say 'children,' say 'daughters'!" For those who intentionally advocate a rediscovery of "women's wisdom," the lesson is obvious: Who knows that death is a part of life? Women. Who refuses to admit this, and instead murderously turn on others to prove their own invulnerability to death? Men, especially soldiers. By extension, those doctors who use the military imagery are also participants in its threat, its blindness to the feminine alternative perspective, not to mention the human needs of patients. While dying "naturally" is what death is really about, death in warfare can tell us nothing. The experiences of dying patients count, while those of soldiers could not—by this logic, at least—tell us anything except the ravages of denial on self and others.

I have stated this argument in its starkest and most simplified form. Unfortunately, it has often been allowed to pervade discussions about death and dying without being stated at all, let alone examined critically. Once stated, it becomes apparent how a nostalgia for "death at home" connects to a feminine sphere in which home is secure and valid, while the world outside is impersonal and cold at best, and at worst dangerous and disordered. A death that is natural, like birth, is an intrinsically embodied and material part of human life, and women are the supposed experts on such matters, while men wish for transcendence and dominion and knowledge apart from the body. Women are the caretakers of the dying, and it is their task to be present as nurturing mother-substitutes for the hospital patients, while the (mostly masculine) doctors are not so much caretakers as scientific warriors, in denial about their own deaths and ready to place the burden of this on their patients. We miss the full impact of Kübler-Ross and the death awareness movement if we overlook how these dichotomized images operate as an intrinsic aspect of the spread of this language. In the post-Vietnam era, a revulsion against automatic glorification of traditionally masculine imagery for warfare has made this connection between the battlefield and the hospital seem plausible. While Americans wanted a "war on cancer," the actual situations of the dying seemed to resemble the war in Vietnam in its most morally problematic aspects. "Nature" and a return of respect for feminine values seemed a valid solution.

As a bit of evidence in favor of this view, we might imagine what shape a rediscovery of death and dying could have taken had the gender distinctions pointed in a different direction. Suppose that to face the bare natural fact of one's own death was a courageous, manly, conscious choice, very different from the gentle evasions and denials that polite, genteel, "feminine" proprieties demanded? We have a hint of how this might have worked, in an unusual first-person narrative, *The Death of a Man*. Author Lael Wertenbaker wrote in the late 1950s of the death of her husband, who, she proudly tells us, was once mistaken for Hemingway at a bullfight. "Wert" died like a man; he was a realist and, although a loving husband, was thoroughly unsentimental about his own impending death. His adoring wife is proud that he knew about his prognosis and planned his suicide carefully. He wanted to be in control up through the very end, and so he was. The local people in the French village where the couple lived were in awe of a man who knew he would die; that was unheard of, too much for an ordinary person to bear. " 'He knows!' they said to each other, over and over, then, and still say it now: 'He knew!' "[16] (Remember that this comes from the memory of his adoring widow, not from an anthropologist's account of dying in rural France.) It may be important that Wert did not let the cancer "get him," that he got to himself first. Is this "natural" death at all?

It is not natural death as the death awareness movement a decade later began to define it, not so much because of the suicide, but because of the drastically different imagery. It might have been possible to be this heroic and macho in the 1950s, but in the middle of the Vietnam era, the same images would have appeared deeply problematic. While the love and admiration of the widow who gives us Wert's story is and remains real, almost every other aspect of the story depends upon a "man's" perspective, a coding of death in terms as far as possible from the feminine. Perhaps those who mistook the protagonist for Hemingway were not too far off the mark, and perhaps the bullfight—a heroic test of manly courage—is the proper image for the story. In any case, it is significant that advocates of natural death did not choose to pick up on these images.

I have posed the argument over gender imagery as a choice focused on *imagery,* on the hidden connotations of ideas and concepts. It is not an argument over the gender balance of hospital or hospice staffs, nor about the preponderance of women over men in certain helping professions. That both men and women find the idea of death as natural appealing and believable suggests that the imagery does not divide rigidly along actual gender lines. On the other hand, the imagery of the death awareness movement has helped locate its advocates within the fields of caretaking and helping rather than principally of scientific research. The question for us, looking back on this post-Vietnam ethos in which the movement flourished, is to ask if continued reluctance to use military imagery, and ongoing preference for "nature," has impeded or aided the movement's ability to say meaningful and comprehensive things about the roles of death in human existence. Can we move beyond or outside these choices and so come to a more adequate assessment of images for death?

V.

In a discussion of death as natural, one must look for the model of the human person presupposed by those who invoke the language of nature and acceptance. If death is natural, yet the person is far more than a biological organism, who or what is such a being? How does this person relate to nature as an entity? The language of the death awareness movement may be used by nonpsychologists, but it has been primarily a psychological one, geared to thinking about individual persons as psychic entities. It has been individualistic rather than drawn from systems theory. It has, by and large, been asociological. The most important thing to see at work in the death awareness movement is the eclipse of psychoanalytic perspectives by those more congruent with a growth model, even when specific concepts such as defense mechanisms seem to be drawn from Freud or his followers. This transition is not an event isolated from the other developments in American psychology during the decades from the late 1960s. In almost every practical therapeutic field, the prestige of psychoanalysis waned from what it had been in the 1950s, and other models and ideals replaced it. When Kübler-Ross edited a volume with the title, *Death: The Final Stage of Growth,* this changeover was already apparent.[17] "Growth" in this sense is not a Freudian category. Yet if death is natural, as natural as birth, then it can in some sense be "growth"; what is needed is a psychological model that allows us to say this. For those who wonder why *Death: the Final Stage of Decay* might not be more appropriate as a title, imagine how a book with such a title could have sold any copies at all since the 1960s. An organic model of growth-minus-decay may in its own way be a denial of death, but it is this growth model that came to pervade the death awareness movement.

What makes Freudian thinking inappropriate for this message? In a Freudian perspective on almost any kind of human experience there are always two forces at work, and they are always in conflict. In most psychoanalytic writings the major conflicts are between desire and reality or between love and hate. No matter what the human situation, a psychoanalytic perspective on it will invoke such conflicts. The person's actual lived behavior will be a compromise between two warring forces, currents, or agencies within the self. Indeed, the whole point of some Freudian thought is to break away from a concept of self so as to avoid all images of unity, wholeness, completeness. As the self is severed into id, ego, and superego—or unconscious, preconscious, and conscious—or pleasure principle versus reality principle, so the "we" who thought we knew who "we" were, vanishes into a multiplicity of powers and agencies, struggling against one another. Moreover, the past dominates these conflicts; the timelessness of the unconscious sees to that. There is no room here for a progressive force deep within the self, only for endless battles that, if won, may stall or limit regression.

In the case of psychoanalytic thought about death, Freud himself developed a language of warring instincts—eros versus thanatos, life versus death. This he described as his own mythology. But American psychoanalysis never adopted this strategy, and stuck instead to a view that Freud had maintained earlier, and that appears in *The Future of an Illusion*. The idea of death is itself unthinkable, and so we create illusory, wishful fantasies to deny it. Denial takes the form of "the illusion of a future," in the phrasing of Avery Weisman.[18] The struggle to break through illusion may be an impossible one, and the very best that can be achieved is a kind of stoic rational recognition that illusions are illusions, based on wish and not reality. Theories such as this do not allow for hope as a psychological principle, to serve as a guide toward resolution. Hope would clearly be another manifestation of denial, of the unconscious as wishful, as the enemy of reality. In this context, acceptance of death means grim resignation, and has none of the hopeful or peaceful qualities given it by Kübler-Ross and others in the death awareness movement. It is no surprise that what Freud has to say about nature here is utterly at odds with the benevolent harmonious imagery we have pointed out; nature is a frustrating, disappointing, cruel enemy that defeats us in the end.

The distance of the psychoanalytic framework—its model of the self and its ethic—from what the death awareness movement means by "death is natural" is therefore very great. The self is hardly a self at all, but a collection of competing agencies, and the vocabulary of "growth," "wholeness," and "self-actualization" is conspicuously absent from psychoanalysis. During the 1970s these terms became the core themes of the human potential movement, the general term for a widespread popularization of the ideas of humanistic psychologists such as Maslow and Rogers, and of activities such as sensitivity groups, encounter weekends, and so forth. The human potential movement used a model of "growth" as an internal, spontaneous process toward fulfillment of built-in biological and psychological potentials; it advocated growth as an ethical and spiritual ideal. This diffused such ideas so widely and firmly into American perspectives that it is hardly surprising that they became present throughout the death awareness movement's expressions. Only in the light of such imagery could death ever be construed as "the final stage of growth," but to get to this point requires some other shifts as well.

The growth model presumes that conflict is not endemic and inevitable, but an accidental and external obstacle. Society or one's parents can impede growth, but the individual is born to grow; he or she will grow and develop without artificial inducements and training. Imagine a bonsai tree, which remains stunted precisely because it is artificially pruned and bound. While it may be more beautiful than a natural, full-grown tree, it is a kind of freak. Of course, no one wants to become a bonsaied person. The growth model makes abundant use of the language of "potential," capacities that will be "actualized" (in the thought of Abraham Maslow, the whole process of growth was "self-actualization"). In the language of the model itself, growth "happens naturally" and is impossible to stop. But in the ethic based on this model, we are morally obligated to actualize our potentials, else we will remain stunted, half-developed as persons. To be natural is to grow as fully and as completely as possible. To die naturally is to experience the final stage of growth. This has changed from a bare statement about the human lifespan into what sounds like an ethical obligation.

But which potential shall I actualize? In what priority? Moreover, how do I identify a potential within myself? If death is such a potential, as the above statements make it sound, then do I have a goal-directed urge to die? That sounds too much like Freud's death instinct, and such an idea never appears in the growth model's discourse at all. Potentials are not something we struggle against; this is not a conflict-based model. We struggle to turn potentials into reality because only this way can we become complete—who we truly are and are meant naturally to be. A creative talent seems to be the obvious example of this, such as the talent for dance or music or drawing. Maslow's self-actualizing persons are generally those who seem to have engaged in particular pursuits with passion and discipline over long periods of time and with a sacrifice of other capacities and interests. This, however, is never how self-actualization is described in his psychological writings that tout it as an ideal. Terms such as "passion," "discipline," and "sacrifice" suggest choices and commitments, very far from the imagery of natural organic growth. Besides, Maslow insisted that the creativity of which he spoke was not just that of musicians and artists, but of those who practice "creative living"; it is therefore available to all.[19] If potential and self-actualization are this democratic, this universal, then they are also comparatively effortless in that the enormous sacrifices made by one who embarks on a career as a professional dancer are irrelevant to the psychological model.

When this picture of the self triumphs culturally, as it did in the 1960s and 1970s, it dramatically mobilizes conflicts between psychological language and other ideals. Such psychological models as Maslow and the human potential movement extolled and advocated seemed to some nothing more than a cult of self-worship.[20] The sustained attack on "expressive individualism" found in Robert Bellah et al.'s *The Habits of the Heart,* is actually an attack on the ethical inadequacies of individual growth and self-actualization as a grounding for actions in society.[21] The argument is that to legitimate one's choices with a language of pseudobiological images of "growth" and "potentials" is to avoid awareness of the effects and quality of those choices. Most often "growth" is a fancy way to justify doing what one wants at the moment, regardless of the pain and inconvenience to others. It provides no guarantee that in the future something different cannot be chosen using the same logic. It is individualistic and selfish, making it all but impossible for persons to acknowledge their obligations to others and the commitments that tie persons together and require sustenance over time. The only real obligation accepted by the expressive individualism of the human potential movement was the obligation to self-actualize. This is what interviewees in Bellah's study seem to have appropriated as their first language, even when their experiences cry out for something more adequate.

This language of growth, natural potentials, and self-fulfillment was available as a replacement for psychoanalysis at the time of the death awareness movement's beginning, and it is this language that has continued to provide a primary, although not exclusive, vocabulary for it. Even when the experiences discussed are of care and relationship, the psychological model is most regularly one of individual growth and development of capacities lying at the heart of a unified self. This accounts for the fact that although death is seen as natural, the contemporary literature does not want to make it seem the same for everyone. Each person grows into herself, each one of us is a unique individual, growing toward her fulfillment. Therefore, each person's death is unique, a final stage for her that cannot be a blueprint for all others. Whatever the organic and biological imagery of growth, in this psychological model it did not operate to reduce persons to identical organisms, but sponsored their individuality, with the consequences that Vitz, Bellah, and others found so objectionable.

Curiously, this ethic of growth and individuality ran into conflict over the most famous attempt to formulate how death is a natural process, the final stage of growth. I mean, of course, the "five stages" of dying proposed by Kübler-Ross. This supposed sequence of denial, anger, bargaining, depression, and acceptance has long been abandoned as an adequate framework within the death awareness movement, but has been honored as an attempt to describe and give form to something previously shunned. This model was often perceived as a blueprint, and objected to because it put everyone into a box; it seemed to restrict persons to one pathway and ideal. Kübler-Ross vigorously denied this; the goal is to make sure each patient dies in his or her own way, at his or her own pace. The most fundamental obligation is to be oneself, near death as earlier in life; to grow into selfhood is an ethical ideal overriding even the counselor's desire to see all patients reach "acceptance." If death is indeed *The Final Stage of Growth,* then what matters is the fulfillment of individual selfhood.

In a study of this feature of the death awareness movement, Bonnie Miller-McLemore found this stress on individualism, the absolute right of everyone to die in a manner fulfilling to himself, one of the marks of its ethical bankruptcy.[22] Mirroring criticisms of the growth model as a whole, Miller-McLemore noted how, far from resolving real conflicts between family and dying patient, or real choices in pathways of conduct, this ethic more or less avoids them. If the only norm is that everyone should follow an individual ethic of growth, does that in practice mean that anything the dying patient wants should be granted because it is an expression of a final growth? Perhaps the popularity of this language is only comprehensible because it is patient advocacy language, and in the milieu of the hospital it demands that doctors and other professionals listen to the patient's voice and start to see things from his or her perspective. As an ethic on its own, however, it is inadequate and incomplete.

Why is the growth model, which undergirds so much of the "death is natural" imagery and ideal, a poor framework for thinking about human experiences of dying? Miller-McLemore and Bellah attack it, but the most thorough formulation of the problems with it as an ethic come from the work of Don Browning. His *Religious Thought and the Modern Psychologies* tackles this in the context of a survey of how psychological theories have functioned as religious and ethical norms in American society. Browning's argument against the growth model is not that it is selfish, but that it assumes an unstated, invalid, and unexamined premise. The model itself claims that growth is an internal drive, that we are meant to self-actualize, and that to prevent or stymie self-actualization is wrong (the bonsai image). But self-actualization operates at the level of individuals; it makes sense only because growth is natural to individual organisms. We cannot, in this theory, speak of an institution, a society, or a species "growing" and mean by this the same fulfilling of its biological and psychological potential as the theory attributes to individuals. What then happens when each individual in fulfillment of his or her potentials, runs into conflict with other individuals intent on the fulfillment of *their* potentials?

Why were the human potential movement and all its spin-offs so silent on this possibility?

The answer, says Browning, is that they made an assumption that no real conflict would occur because, in the larger picture, no one's interests truly conflict. Each self-actualizer is complementary to every other self-actualizer; all eventually will harmonize in a wider system of noncompeting, mutually interlocking aims. This is the invisible hand of the free market; it is the postulating of an inherently harmonious self-correcting complex system, where in the long run there will be enough room for all to fulfill their individual needs. Such a "hidden harmony" assures us that if we pursue our own interests single-mindedly, others will do so too and we will not have to worry that they and we will ever have to compromise.[23]

When it is put this way, as a rational proposition about the world, such an assumption of a hidden harmony behind all individual aims is so blatantly false that it is very rarely ever stated so plainly. In fact, in the psychological literature I have never seen this argument spelled out in this fashion. As Browning notes, it is a hidden assumption, which allows self-actualization theory to bypass the tricky questions of actual moral conduct and choices. Maslow just didn't think it was necessary to discuss these since my growth cannot truly interfere with yours, when both are adequately recognized as natural pathways of each individual organism. Most often the expressions of this idea are even more veiled, so that "Follow your bliss!" and other slogans of the human potential movement result, and sound like ethical injunctions. Whatever this means, it sounds a lot better than what Browning unpacks as its meaning philosophically. To the extent that growth models used as comprehensive ethical systems play a role in the death awareness movement, they may not always sound so obvious as this, or as "death is the final stage of growth," but they are present nevertheless. Those who allow such models to dominate their thinking about persons, almost without exception include the assumption of hidden harmony even when they venture into areas of debate where other principles of choices and values must be included.

What makes this hidden harmony assumption so intimately tied to the natural death language and imagery we are examining? What is the connection between them, save that the growth model in its psychological expressions systematically employs the former, and the death awareness movement relies upon such psychologies for most of its expressions. There is a closer, less accidental connection. Because that hidden harmony, that system in which all ends can meet and within which no individual's growth is forbidden, is Nature, the mythical ideal of Nature that death awareness movement language connotes. Within Nature as an ecological system, there is a harmony of sorts, there is a mutual balance between one's aims and another's. Within this system, death belongs, and so is acceptable. The invocation of this mythical imagery is one of the factors that allows the ethical limits of the growth model to persist unchecked and unnoticed. Once again, when we or others today invoke Nature in this manner, we are not thinking of Darwin's "nature red in tooth and claw," but of a system that works to establish harmony, balance, inclusiveness. In contrast, Browning is saying that real life is indeed filled with conflicts, "red in tooth and claw" and unresolvable without further ethical principles to guide us.

But what is the flaw in this? Is it only that Nature is too unreal, that it lacks all reference to competition and predation? No, there is another problem. The point of view has been shifted from that of the individual (who grows and self-actualizes) to a larger unit—Nature as ecological system. An ecological system may be harmonious, and the system has places for an immense variety of creatures. But that does not guarantee that any one organism will survive for more than a single minute. In fact, the violent and early deaths of whole classes of specific individuals may be the way the system maintains itself. From the individual creature's perspective, it is little comfort that the system itself will endure, when self, family, and perhaps even one's entire species will vanish. The complementarity of individual self-interests, postulated by growth theories, exists only as a fiction; there is no real guarantee of this, even in the most stable ecological system. Ecologically interdependent Nature cannot provide a mythical backdrop for our own individuality, our own growth or self-actualization, unless this switch in perspectives is overlooked.

It is true that there is room for death in an ecological system; the deaths of individuals, and their replacements by other individuals, are a given. In this sense, natural death makes some sense as an image. But when more is done with the imagery, it fails to guarantee the solution to specific ethical and human problems that its users hope. It can be meaningfully located in the choice between Ivan Ilych and Gerasim, but why then call either one "natural"? What is really being offered is a choice between two human possibilities, one of which is in harmony with nature. Is this the most adequate way to tell the difference between them? As we have just seen, this is to jumble a great many assumptions, juxtaposing a psychological model of unlimited individualism upon an ecological image designed for species living in an environment with other species. The appeal of Nature as a mythical image may be furthered by its gender-identification. But it is also appealing because it sees a realm far from the actual human, high-tech context within which so much modern dying takes place. To make better sense of the death awareness movement and its agenda, we must turn to that context. There the problems and issues that shape and are reshaped by the new language for dying and death will be most apparent.

MEDITATION 2: ACCEPTANCE
Matthew 27:50; Luke 23:46

"And when Jesus had cried out again in a loud voice, he gave up his spirit."

"Jesus called out with a loud voice, 'Father, into your hands I commit my spirit.'"

There is no sign of "natural death" here, and it is pointless to look for it amid the narrative of a public execution. What we may receive instead is a different ideal: yielding of one's spirit to God. This is a voluntary, intended act, Jesus' last act according to both these Gospels. This will be a way for us to read "acceptance" into the passion, and to link its message and images to our own lives and deaths.

At the time of his arrest, Jesus told Peter to put away the drawn sword. "Do you think I cannot call on my Father, and he will at once put at my disposal more than twelve legions of angels?" (Matt. 26:53). Renunciation of military prowess, of victory through force, is at once both physical and spiritual. This is the stance of Jesus consistently throughout the passion. Yielding, giving up to God, is the consummation of this. It is not passive, but it is intentionally non-heroic, noncombative. The twelve legions of angels remain on call, waiting, but they are never summoned. This is the choice that creates the space for Jesus' acceptance of his death. It is the Father's will for him to die, and without this death, the scriptures would remain unfulfilled. This is Matthew's way of insisting that Jesus' last acts be placed within God's long-term plan. It is this plan's ultimate goodness that sustains Jesus to the end.

Jesus accepts his own particular death, coming at this time and in this horrible manner. His readiness to give up his spirit may have surprised his enemies; sometimes victims lived several days on their crosses. Had Jesus struggled against death, encountered it as an enemy to be conquered or humiliated, he might have lasted longer. As Wert Wertenbaker exclaims: "My God, it takes a hell of a lot to kill a man!"[25] Wert never surrendered; even his suicide was an assertion of his will and his self-determination. But then, if for Jesus this kind of personal victory or conquest had been the aim, those twelve legions of angels were on hand.

Before the start of his public ministry, Jesus was tempted over what kind of kingdom he was to proclaim. Would it be based on spectacular miracles of world domination or wish fulfillment? No, none of these. At the end, the same choice is still there. Those twelve legions of angels represent the road not taken when Jesus refused to throw himself from the top of the temple and count on God for miraculous rescue. There is no such victory in his kingdom, no last minute escape from the cross. Had it been otherwise, the kingdom of God would have appeared with blazing letters in the sky, worldly rule and power guaranteed. With this, who God is and how God acts in the world would have been utterly different. Yes, there are miraculous rescues and reprieves in the scriptures, but this time, God is not going to work this way.

Jesus surrenders—to God the Father, not to death as a personified enemy, or to his human judges and captors. He will not fight to stay alive. His timing is right, his death is not premature. Although there is nothing natural about his ending, there is indeed a sense of fittingness and appropriateness in his own eyes and in that of the narratives.

But what about the resurrection? Reading this death through the lens of the resurrection, the church soon reverses some of the imagery. The military conquest language reemerges. "Having disarmed the powers and authorities, he made a public spectacle of them, triumphing over them by the cross" (Col. 2:15). It is not Jesus who endures defeat and humiliation, but the spiritual powers hostile to him. These spiritual powers (demonic? worldly authorities?) are treated as the Romans dealt with all defeated enemies, parading them in humiliating chains in a giant victory procession. If this is what really happened at Calvary, it is not Jesus who is unarmed and vulnerable, but his enemies. The cross is triumph, not a place for his surrender. A cosmic military struggle did occur after all, although the visible events could not be read this way except through the eyes of faith. Jesus conquered death the enemy, not through twelve legions of angels, but nevertheless effectively for all time. Although it may be crude to equate these "powers and authorities" with biological death, we may find here the source for Cullman's twentieth-century retelling. Against this background, it is hard to see "acceptance," let alone "natural death," as anything but pagan, alien to the Christian vision of God triumphant.

But this is to ignore what seems to be the more direct meaning of the Gospels: Jesus intended his death, he is able to let go of his life when the time comes for him to do so. He relinquishes not only his life, but military models for what happens to him, and for what God wants in this situation. While we cannot claim that Jesus dies in what Kübler-Ross would consider a state of acceptance, we need not pit the entire Christian vision of death against such hopes. There is an opposition in the passion narrative, but it is to a kingdom inaugurated and maintained by force, human or angelic. In the space this leaves, Jesus willingly yields his spirit on the cross, not as an act of defeat or victory in regard to death, but an act of trust in his Father.

The Contemporary Setting: Medicalization vs. the "Whole Person"

I.

When Ivan Ilych was dying at home in 1886, he was visited and treated by a series of doctors who denied him truth and humanity. Their contribution to his plight was insistence that his problems were medical. "A kidney or an appendix?" not "life or death?" was their framework, their way to avoid real encounter with both the patient and with death. Tolstoy clearly believes the medical perspective tells us nothing worth knowing about the meaning of our lives, our deaths, ourselves. Why, then, did the medical perspective so captivate Ivan? He barely questions any of his doctors about what they do or do not deign to tell him. He acquiesces to their expertise, although finally in fury he refuses to believe their lies. This account precedes the high-tech hospital. It is as if the human scene is already set for this development; the attitudes of the protagonists are all in place, ready for the emergence of medicine and hospitals as we know them, places where dying can happen under scientific-medical auspices. Read from this perspective, what the death awareness movement labels the pervasive denial of death in modern society comes first; it then creates the kind of institutions that will express and perpetuate "wild death," however much we who come afterwards may protest this. Were Tolstoy to come back to life and walk through a hospital, he might say that Ivan's heirs created for themselves a realm congruent to their pervasive inauthenticity. This is a realm in which death is present but denied, in which "It" holds unacknowledged power precisely because "It" is unacknowledged except as a medical condition.

This perspective reverses what is the most usual outlook on hospitals and medicine and death. The death awareness movement's most common claim is that thanks to the advances of twentieth-century medicine we have cured diseases, but at the same time isolated ourselves from the dying. Our impersonal, bureaucratic, technological hospitals are geared for the treatment and cure of acute illness through better technology and continuing research into the biological causes of disease. Medicine's heroic successes have come through such institutions. The problem is that within such a setting, death is automatically defined as failure to cure, as a failure on the part of the doctor and perhaps even the patient. It is high-tech medicine and the hopes it inspires that make death unacceptable. It is the hospital setting that makes for the isolation, loneliness, and despair of the dying. Such arguments, as we have already seen, have overwhelmed the (Freudian) concern to prove that death has always been denied, always been feared, and projected away from ourselves. Indeed, the hospital setting is itself to blame for the ignorance of dying on the part of most persons; we no longer see death as part of ordinary life, for it is isolated and technologized. Although the exact percentage of persons who die in hospitals varies from decade to decade (from about 50 percent of the deaths in 1950 to about 80 percent in 1970 and then down to 75 percent in 1980), what seems to remain is the medicalization of dying. Medical doctors are those whose expertise reigns, who define what it means to die. Thus, the dying person becomes "the terminally ill patient," even in the contemporary literature intent on protesting this medicalization.

If there is one fact that separates today's death and dying from that of the religious traditions, it is medicalization. Indeed, it separates North American dying and death from that of societies whose medicine is not of the Western scientific variety. The questions our medicine asks about dying focus on disease, on the physical condition of the body; its categories are those of diagnosis, treatment, and prognosis. As we have seen, these terms play no role at all in the perspectives familiar to Christians in the past. Neither the *Ars Moriendi* nor *The Pilgrim's Progress* nor any other traditional Christian guidebook for living and dying ever defined the dying person's plight in medical categories. Doctors and their remedies had a role to play, but it was insignificant at the ultimate level. Do we even think to ask what disease forced Christian, Mr. Stand-fast, and the rest into the river that leads to the Heavenly City? Of course not. While today, the dying hospital patient begins from a medicalized perspective on what is happening, and may or may not be able to develop an alternative to supplement this.

The past and the present seem completely discontinuous here. No theologian or devotional writer in the past—and this includes everyone until the twentieth century's "wild death" era—ever started from medicalized death. The questions of treatment, prognosis, pain control, alternative medicines such as homeopathy, may all have been real questions, but they were not the dominant questions. For us, however, they are. It seems impossible to bypass these entirely. The struggle is to get beyond them, or to discover human meanings that go beyond the medical meanings. This is not a task traditional writers faced, and this is the purpose of almost all contemporary writings on death and dying from the death awareness movement. The medicalization of death has therefore required dramatically reshaped visions of what spiritual care for the dying requires. How does the language of faith and spirituality fit into the medicalized understanding? How does the representative of the body of Christ—whether chaplain, visiting pastor, or ordinary layperson—fit within the bureauratic hospital? Is it a matter of religion versus science, of a faith perspective contrasted with a secular approach to knowledge? Or do such divisions not fit the situation? The medicalized framework was never intended to be so comprehensive and all-pervading as it has become. Its weaknesses and gaps demand some additional vision, imagery, and set of meanings, even if not necessarily those that are identifiably "religious."

If the popular claim is oversimplified that Western scientific medicine and the modern hospital setting cause denial of death, the practice of Western medicine carries along with it a cluster of attitudes, roles, and problems wherever it goes. Hospitals organize the segregation of the sick from the healthy, for reasons that make sense medically but have unintended human consequences. Among these are the isolation of the dying from the rest of society and the avoidance of death by the healthy. Medicine gives to doctors the final say, for it is their knowledge and authority that count. But this recognition of their valid medical expertise extends into realms such as ethics, where they are not necessarily experts, and where they should not necessarily have the final say. Within the basic framework of Western medicine, then, two problems work ravages that the death awareness movement tries to repair: patients' sense of isolation and their loss of moral control over their own fates. Although Ivan Ilych suffered both of these problems, they are vastly intensified by the modern high-tech hospital milieu. In response to these problems, the death awareness movement has joined with other voices to remind all that although the doctor is expert on the diseased body, there is a *whole person* at stake. This whole person needs a voice, either his or her own or that of an advocate. Care for the whole person is a theme intended to overcome both isolation and the loss of moral control. Within this struggle, "wild death" as pervasive and intensified denial of death emerges. It is intrinsic to medicalized death.

A case can be made that wherever Western scientific medicine takes over a society, its attitudes toward dying will be reshaped so as to resemble those found in Western society: to deny death, silence it, and so create wild death even when nothing like this had been present before. A society such as traditional Japan did not deny death, and all accounts by Westerners who observed this society prior to its rapid transition to modern Japan noted how death was not avoided or feared. Some found the Japanese "death obsessed," while others noted that Buddhist influences left persons, even children, concerned about the prospect of their friends' deaths, but not fundamentally frightened of their own.[1] The result of the triumph of Western medicine in contemporary Japan is a version of wild death so virulent that the Westerners who observe it find it unbearable. Medicalized death in Japan now takes the form of never telling the terminal patient the diagnosis, never using the word "cancer," never directly communicating vital information about treatments and prognosis, and forcing families to comply with this vow of silence. A harrowing account of such a terminal illness is told by Clayton Naff, an American journalist whose Japanese father-in-law lies dying of cancer in a hospital. Naff cannot believe that this is what people want, that the loving family will endure this deception. To him, the loss of relationship and moral control are an intolerable breach of the very dignity they all struggle to maintain.

> In my most morbid fantasies, I have sometimes wondered how I would spend my last days if I knew I had a fatal disease. Many variations had played through my head. . . . But never in all my imaginings had it occured to me that I might be condemned without being told. . . . It was just too monstrous to conceive.[2]

The irony here is that Naff forgets that this was exactly the normal situation of Americans less than thirty years before he wrote. He forgets that this vow of silence once was considered the only way to protect the patient from knowledge too horrendous to handle. By 1994, this was already a foreign idea to him, but in Japan Western medicine had effectively replicated the 1950s of North America, had effectively shut out the traditional culture, which made space for death. Having taken over the management of dying, and reregulated its language, Western scientific medicine has left the Japanese just as miserable, isolated, and powerless as Americans were at the time the death awareness movement took shape.

In the wake of this takeover by scientific medicine and the hospital milieu come certain strategies of protest. Most of these accept the basic framework of medicalization, but reject the indignity of patients' loss of control. The call to engage in more "holistic," "whole person" understandings of the patient express this protest. Other protest strategies emerge in the shadow of the medical model and parallel it chronologically. The twentieth century may go on record as the era of fascination with spiritual healing, for many movements in and outside of Christianity focused on inclusion of medicalized concern for bodily health within a wider or at least a different perspective. Pentecostalism and the charismatic movement within Christianity led more traditional Christian denominations into rites of healing, seemingly a response to a grassroots interest. Many of the "new" and "new new" (post-1970) religious groups in Japan also center on healing, not coincidentally. A focus on healing itself seems derivative from the medical model, as in the presentation of the gospel as "God's health plan." (Yes, I actually heard this expression used, as a standard image in charismatic circles in southern California!) This is not an alternative to medicine, at least not in most cases; it can best be grasped as an attempt to claim back from medicine a different vision of what being sick means as a human experience. But such spiritual perspectives remain outside the primary focus of the death awareness movement and this book. My concern is to locate the death awareness movement in a wider context of response to medicalization, a response that basically works within the system of hospitals, high-technology, and medical categories, but wants to maintain that these alone are inadequate.

II.

I have identified isolation and loss of moral authority as the two basic problems faced by patients within the situation of medicalization. How has the death awareness movement tried to respond to these? And what is the role of Christian faith once medicalization is firmly in place? It is here that a firm alliance between the death awareness movement and Christians, particularly "official" voices such as those of hospital chaplains, emerges. At the level of protest on behalf of "the whole person" and "the patient's perspective," there is no substantive disagreement between the death awareness movement and Christian perspectives, whatever the fundamental divergence of imagery for death. Indeed, long before the death awareness movement of the 1960s and 1970s, Christian voices spoke on behalf of patients, against "the evils of specialism" in hospital care, and advocated concern for the whole person.[3] Chaplains noted how loneliness and helplessness made the physical aspects of illness worse, and yet medicine seemed to ignore and exclude what it could not itself cure. Forms of mental and spiritual pain thus went unrecognized. When the patient recovered he or she could leave the hospital and get back to ordinary life, regaining relationships and moral control. For the dying, alas, no such escape from medicine's stronghold seemed possible.

To strengthen the patient's sense of control, of moral agency, is a goal all death awareness movement advocates share. One might expect that, when patients could not speak for themselves, family members or friends would take on this role for them. But here the isolation of hospital patients contributes to their helplessness. The family has gone home after visiting hours; it is not an intimate of the hospital environment. The hospital chaplain is, and so he or she takes on the role of patient advocate, if not legally then morally, reminding the medical specialists that there is a person at the center of their efforts. It is the chaplain who can become communicator of the human dimensions of illness, not just for the patient but for others in the medical setting.

To accomplish this, those who minister to the sick are advised to be present, to listen, to respect, and to attend to the person as a whole person. This advice is offered not only by and for chaplains but for all who find themselves as Christ's representatives in the hospital setting. Aimed at overcoming isolation and loss of moral authority, it is the most often repeated material in pastoral care literature dealing with death, just as in the death awareness movement as a whole. It is the cliché of every "how to" book on the subject. A suspicious person might wonder if the need to repeat this simple advice so frequently is a sign that it is regularly disregarded. It is certainly evidence of the immense pressure medicalization puts on those who want to maintain that the patient as whole person comes first.

What is there to prevent chaplains from sliding into the role of being one more specialist, this one a religious expert? Indeed, specialism has affected ministry as well as other areas of life, so that tasks all Christians could accomplish for each other have frequently been linked solely to the specialized professional role of hospital chaplain. When a chaplain admits that her chief delight is to gain access to patients' medical files, and that this was a strong part of her motivation for going into hospital ministry, one sees how the allure of specialized insider knowledge can corrupt even those who ought to be alert to this danger. The literature is filled with complaints about chaplains who hide behind prayer and Bible reading, and so create for themselves roles as religious experts while ignoring the patient as a whole person. Not that prayer and Bible reading are themselves evil, but when these are joined to a persona of religious specialist, the basic human problems created by medicalization are not solved.

A clear example of the moral problems of medicalization and the ambiguous role of chaplains in handling these, is a 1997 essay by Anne Simmonds on "Pastoral Perspectives in Intensive Care: Experiences of Doctors and Nurses with Dying Patients," published in the *Journal of Pastoral Care*. Simmonds states that the deaths of patients in the ICU create a tremendous sense of failure for the staff. The medical model makes cure the goal, and death is defined as failure to cure. Consequently, the medical perspective itself leads to overtreatment. This occurs even against the desires of the patients' families, and the private better judgment of the staff. But the chaplain can stand for an alternative vision.

> This study confirms that patients are sometimes cared for in a way that strips them of their humanity. The chaplain is a presence which reminds others of the importance of the whole person and the respect that each person deserves, even if they are unable to speak for themselves.[4]

Medicalization of dying creates a group of specialists intent on "doing"—and in some cases "overdoing"—while the chaplain seems to focus more on "being."[5] His presence is potentially salutory precisely because he is focused on the whole person, on claims and meanings and values that exceed the medical perspective. He is not a specialist dealing with religion, but one who can communicate with families better than any of the specialists, provide emotional support for staff, and raise issues of dying and death from outside the medical framework. Here again the moral problems of isolation and loss of control within the hospital setting itself shape the behavior of all within its landscape. The ICU merely intensifies these problems present within the whole landscape of medicalization.

Although Simmonds writes as a Christian about the role of chaplain, her perspective completely converges with that of the death awareness movement. Both voices insist that the patient as a whole person ought to come first. To listen to the patient is the foremost moral obligation of all who work to alleviate fear, helplessness, and loneliness. "It is important to *follow the patient's agenda*."[6] This is repeated in pastoral care literature and in all death awareness writings as a message to all who are concerned with the human consequences of medicalization.

True, the contemporary death awareness movement does not start as a Christian protest against the ICU situation. It begins as a secular psychological movement, which, as we saw, uses naturalistic imagery for death. But that hides the other half of the story. Recall that Elisabeth Kübler-Ross began her seminar with seminary students, and her most consistent and positive relationships were with hospital chaplains. Her own naturalistic perspective in *On Death and Dying* makes it easy to overlook this early alliance. When a movement was born that escaped the categories of scientific thanatology (a subspecialty of psychiatry, and thus of medicine), chaplains and clergy played and continue to play a role in the spread of its ideas. Only when chaplains retreat into the role of religious specialist is there any divergence in the message. Therefore, rather than think (as we did in chapters 1 and 2) of "Christian" versus "naturalistic" perspectives on death, we should revision the landscape and the options it offers. There is the medicalized

understanding, which remains dominant from at least the time of
Ivan Ilych, and then there is an alternative whole person view as a
subordinate, complementary protest against the dominant approach. The latter's advocates claim that it alone can alleviate the
mental and spiritual anguish the medical view leaves in its wake,
and for which it can provide no cure. The important thing to note is
how the entire discussion leaves the dominance of the medical
framework as the primary fact, and fits the whole person alternative
into a small yet crucial slot in the midst of medicine's domain.

This creates a subtle double bind for Christians concerned with
the medicalization of death, and how to respond to it. To the extent that specialism and narrowly defined models of expertise are
part of the problem, the Christian role will be to go beyond these
and affirm patients as whole persons in the face of hospital pressures against this. But if this role is to be *Christian,* then there
ought to be some references to the distinctively faith-centered
quality of the chaplain or whoever else comes to the hospital representing Christ's presence. "I put on my cross to let people know
why I'm there," said one hospital visitor. Recovery of separate
Christian identity does not appear as a concern until after the first
enthusiastic wave of endorsements for the death awareness movement by chaplains and pastoral caregivers. Indeed, for many who
work in hospitals it never becomes an issue at all. The injunction
to follow the patients' own agendas takes priority over any faith
concerns of the Christian visitor.

Yet Christian presence amid medicalization seems to require
something more than this. If the task of the Christian is to affirm the
patient's status as a whole person, then the one who ministers to the
sick needs to be recognized as a whole person as well. If faith is truly
part of one's identity, then some space should be made for distinctive perspectives, tasks, and ideals, so as to differentiate the Christian from the secular advocate for the whole person. A return in the
1980s to a focus on distinctive Christian resources for pastoral care
balanced repudiation of the religious specialist model by insisting
that chaplains are not duplicates of social workers, secular counselors, or other nonmedical hospital staff. Religious resources, in-

cluding prayer and Bible reading, have a central place in how chaplains and other Christians combat medicalization.[7] To pray with someone is not inevitably to force a religious agenda upon that person; it is to stress their ultimate identity as a child of God, a mode of whole personhood powerfully different from a lesser identity as hospital patient. Using religious resources wisely enhances the dignity and moral authority of the patient, reduces the sense of isolation, and thus helps undo the evil consequences of medicalization. Such an emphasis does not, therefore, depart from the agenda of the death awareness movement, even if its rationale may sometimes sound like a renewed call for religious specialization.

What is true for chaplains should also apply to lay visitors, fellow members of a congregation, friends, and family. Christian faith is not some kind of alternate specialized knowledge, parallel to that of medicine. It is not the peculiar province of chaplains to represent Christ's presence in the hospital setting. Faith requires, within the context of the hospital, commitment to the patient as a whole person, and so respects the agenda and commitment of that patient. In saying this, I believe that renewed emphasis on the distinctively Christian identity of those who minister to patients may help, rather than distract from, this concern. Still, these approaches to ministering to patients can only alleviate the consequences, rather than prevent medicalization of dying and death.

III.

If medicalization thrives in the high-tech hospital setting, why not solve the problems it creates by removing dying persons from this milieu? Why not create a new kind of place, designed explicitly to combat isolation and loss of moral authority? Better still, why not work to keep the dying in their own homes, where they are close to the people who matter to them, and where they may retain moral if not physical control over their own lives? The death awareness movement embraced both these options. The modern hospice movement entered North America at the same time the

death awareness movement began, and these have been allies in
their hope to change society's attitudes toward death and care of
the dying. To examine hospice in all its aspects is impossible here;
what I will do is comment on how hospice aimed to escape the limits of medicalization, and how it has only very partially succeeded.
Christians who wished for attention to the whole person in the hospital setting have joined with other advocates of hospice, and there
is every reason for them to continue to do so. But hospice by itself
has not been able to reverse medicalization, nor live up to some of
its earlier Utopian hopes to undo the denial of death in society.

The modern hospice movement was founded in the 1960s by
Cecily Saunders, a British physician whose explicit Christian faith
was part of her personal vision for what became, for a while, a
movement. Hospice originated in England, where, due to church-
state ties, a part of the original hospice profile was explicitly religious. Hospice met the problem of specialism by insisting that
dying as a human situation demanded more than one dimension of
meaning. Consequently, a team of specialists pooling expertise is
intrinsic to its method. Moreover, volunteers, who are not experts
in any recognized sense, are just as intrinsic to the hospice model
of care. Relief of physical pain in the form of specialized medication (the "hospice cocktail") went together with the relief of other
forms of pain, equally real: emotional pain, social pain, and spiritual pain were all to be addressed and alleviated. Hospice takes seriously the plight of the whole person and intends to provide an
independent philosophy of care for the whole person when terminally ill. Its aim is for the person to live as fully as possible, even
when the medical prognosis is terminal. This means that one remains recognized as a whole person up until the time of death.
Early accounts of hospice (such as Victor and Rosemary Zorza's
A Way to Die[8]) focused on this outlook and its implications. This
philosophy held that rather than seeing dying as a medical failure,
dying was still human living. Palliative care, medicine focused on
the relief of pain and the comfort of the patient, is its label at the
medical level. But the hospice philosophy provides a great deal
more; it seemed to be a model for the aims Kübler-Ross and so

many others of the death awareness movement hoped to achieve as an alternative to the normal medicalized hospital perspective.

The original ethos of hospice was religious, explicitly Christian. Yet, *A Way to Die,* an autobiographical narrative by the Zorzas about the death of their daughter in an English hospice facility, stresses that the religious dimension of hospice is optional. This is not *just* for the religious; it is an approach that will work for everyone, even the secular Zorzas. The spiritual dimension of hospice care focuses on the genuine love and attention given to their daughter Beth as a unique person, not on anything they or the nurses identify as "religion." Spiritual care was to remain an intrinsic element of hospice, and the National Hospice Organization founded in 1971 insisted that this was a dimension of the total program. However, the pluralism of American society, along with religion's distance from public funding, necessitated a very broad definition of spiritual care.[9] This generates confusion over how spiritual care is given and who gives it, with the result that even by the late 1980s over 90 percent of American hospice programs "failed to demonstrate adequate spiritual care."[10] This statistic shows how vulnerable the nonmedical component of even an intentionally interdisciplinary, "whole person" program is.

An unforeseen development of this conflict was that American hospice became identified with home care, with the move out of the hospital and back into the family environment. This model of hospice is different from the original English blueprint (which became known here as a "free-standing hospice"). Given the problems Simmonds and so many others find endemic to the hospital milieu, what a wonderful and obvious solution! What better place to remain a whole person than in one's own natural setting, one's home? When it became obvious that home care could be much cheaper than any institutional care, insurance companies supported hospice. Home care could be made easier due to certain technical innovations, such as surgically implanted devices for patients to deliver their own pain medication to themselves (they generally require much less medication when it becomes subject to their own control). Moreover, remember that hospice includes team support persons, who can assist the family and alleviate their social isolation and helplessness. True, not all families are suited for such tasks, and some illnesses are not manageable at home, no matter how determined everyone is to avoid hospitalization. But hospice as home care, backed by the philosophy of palliative medicine and a whole person focus, ought to have made an immense and immensely constructive impact on how Americans cope with medicalized death.

Yet that has not occurred. After more than twenty years of hospice care, problems with medicalization still remain. The ICU situation depicted by Simmonds shows little impact of hospice as an alternative way to die. Debates over assisted suicide continue, seemingly without reference to hospice philosophy. Why has hospice not had more of an impact? Is its fate a sign of the failure of the death awareness movement as a whole to shift us away from silence and denial? That would be an overstatement. I believe many advocates for hospice simply underestimated how pervasive the medicalization of death really is.

In order to be a hospice patient, one must be dying, and know that one is dying. A six-month life expectancy is and remains (at the time of my writing) the absolute requirement for admission into hospice programs. Patients and their families who are inveterate deniers will never, even under the best of conditions, be able to cope with the minimal basic awareness that a prognosis is terminal. While a friend timidly recommends hospice, the sick person and her family plan on her attendance at a daughter's high school graduation three months away. In that case, the woman died within a week. Even when the downhill progression of many diseases is well known, this problem of family denial and procrastination remains an obstacle to enrollment in hospice.

Moreover, the same doctors who overtreat in the ICU and who believe a patient's death is a medical failure will often be very reluctant to refer the terminally ill patient to hospice. Even if it is now linked to home care, hospice itself is medicine; it is derivative of the hospital milieu and the medicalization of dying that dominates there. The problems of that environment spill over at many points into the operation of hospice programs. If lack of communication between medical staff, families, and patients remains a problem, then it is unlikely that the presence of hospice can by itself overcome this.

Indeed, in recent years other pressures and problems affecting medicine have affected the impact of hospice and the kind of care it can offer. The same pressures for cost-cutting and self-marketing that now drive hospitals also reshape hospice. The costs of bringing on new patients who live only a few weeks are very high; as this pattern becomes the norm, the programs must be stretched financially. One solution is to recruit new hospice patients among nursing home residents. This may benefit these individuals, but a nursing home has its own problems of isolation and loss of moral authority; it is certainly neither home care, nor the kind of special facility designed for the hospice philosophy that Saunders originally conceived.

Together with financial pressures have come increasingly detailed and strict guidelines about who is eligible for hospice. These are based on a medically set prognosis and medical measures. When these are truly enforced, the medical perspective on disease once again emerges as the controlling one, the language everyone must follow. Because the language of medicine is the language of health care regulation and insurers, it is the one language that works in a climate where everyone needs to be held accountable. Alas, a program whose philosophy aims to discourage a narrowly medical understanding of dying is vulnerable to these pressures. The language of "whole person" and "spiritual care" simply does not carry the same public weight. It cannot be used to regulate, or to assess patients in ways that everyone accepts as objective.

The tale of hospice might be read as a story of secularization from its religious roots via a vague and impotent definition of "spiritual care." It could be read also as a testimony to the power of medicalization and free-market categories. In both these readings, the clear mandate of Christians is to continue to support hospice, both as Christians and as persons continuously struggling to minimize the isolation of the dying and their loss of moral authority. Perhaps medicalization is so firmly in place that an all-out attack upon it will inevitably fail. Therefore, it may be at other levels, and in other ways, that Christians may work more effectively to change attitudes so that whole person care at the end of life is less vulnerable to the demands of specialists and the ICU environment.

There are additional benefits of Christian support for hospice. One is the latter's vision of the person, which is far richer than that of the humanistic psychological language used by most death awareness psychological writers. Hospice is committed to a notion of care that accepts human interdependence and relationship as the norm. Curiously, the psychological models do not themselves encourage this vision, especially those that depend upon an ultra-individualistic view of growth and self-actualization. Hospice works with the whole person as seen within a network of preexisting, nonmedical relationships. The elimination of these from mainstream Western medicine is so pervasive it is rarely noticed; each patient as diseased body is family-less, becoming an isolated atom whose social network is left outside the laboratory, the X-ray room, and the ICU. To the extent that Christians should support any philosophy, practice, or activity aimed at restoring relatedness to our definitions of what it means to be human, hospice is good in itself. The nonrelationality of Western scientific medicine is not spiritually neutral. It is, or has become when medical categories overreach themselves, itself pernicious.

To extend this theme of relationality, Christians should also support hospice's model of care that includes volunteers. Critical illness is a time when families, already under so many pressures in our society, need extrafamilial support. The loneliness and isolation of contemporary hospital patients can become the loneliness and isolation of contemporary family caretakers of the terminally ill. Ivan Ilych lived in a world of servants, and his primary and best caretaker was the young butler's assistant, Gerasim, who was comfortable with both death and illness. Hospice volunteers serve in a very different sense, yet they are also a self-selected population of persons comfortable around the dying and the families of the dying. Their wisdom is not one more form of specialism, but it testifies to a Christian ideal of human linkages beyond family and kinship. Once again, hospice may not by itself be able to displace medicalized death—there is ample evidence that it cannot do so—but there are features of its philosophy and practice that are important. These ought to be supported by Christians, regardless of how little explicitly "Christian" remains in the public language of hospice in America.

Overall, however, almost thirty years of the death awareness movement and hospice programs have not succeeded in overcoming medicalization of death, nor in alleviating the plight of many of the dying and their families. In an attempt to speak against this on behalf of the whole person, it has not really succeeded in changing medical practice very much. Studies such as Simmonds's of the ICU reveal how little Americans' attitudes and our concepts of medicine have changed on these issues. Although death is much more openly discussed than in the 1960s, and the Japanese experiences of complete silence are now viewed as "foreign" rather than normal, one could argue that this part of the original agenda of the death awareness movement has failed. We still medicalize death, we have not developed a real alternative.

IV.

This chapter has discussed settings, institutions, and social roles, instead of private and personal meanings. There is a reason for doing so: *where* something is said, and *who* says it, regularly influences *what* is said. But I am not an institutional determinist. Programs and environments, whether the ICU or the home, are not the whole story. Perhaps even the relational model of the self needs to be supplemented by reaffirming the self's capacity for transcendence and inwardness amid even the most miserable settings. The isolation of Ivan Ilych was not truly undone by his dependence on Gerasim, but instead through an intensely private dialogue with an inner voice, the voice of his soul. This voice asks, "What do you really want?" and guides him into an encounter with the truth about his life.[11] Only when he faces this truth does he stop fearing death. A completely horizontal, relational view of the self leaves out this inwardness, just as medicalization leaves out both the whole person of the patient and the patient's nexus of human ties.

Inwardness and transcendence are human possibilities. They are less visible than programs and environments, and they are not resources in the sense of tools or techniques. But even the sickest hospital patients carry inwardness and transcendence within them into the farthest reaches of the medical setting. The testimonies of many autobiographers is that they, like Ivan, learned in sickness to listen to the voice of the soul. Perhaps because so much pastoral care and death awareness literature is focused on the social task of overcoming medicalization's harms, there is surprisingly little emphasis on this voice and its powers. For instance, prayer appears as an activity of chaplains and other visitors to do with and for the sick. That prayer is already happening when the sick person, alone, cries out to God needs to be affirmed as well. This is implicit in a vision of the whole person, whose inwardness goes beyond what other human beings can know or see. Such a vision of the soul's capacity to be alone with God should never be allowed to languish in favor of a purely relational and horizontal model of the self. To restore it may be a sure defense, albeit a hidden one, against both specialism and medicalization.

Medicalized death remains dominant, and concern for the whole person has not displaced this at the level of public institutions and social settings. Yet, focusing on the whole person bears other fruit. It allows individuals and families to make sense at a private level of their own mortality, and to supply the meanings behind the medicine. The many autobiographies of terminal illness remind us how medicine alone fails to work as a full provider of spiritual food for the whole person. In many of these, spirituality plays a very large role in determining how individuals recast the medical setting and its pressures. Here, the death awareness movement does not seem to have failed, it seems to be part of a way to move beyond "wild death," to speak new and nonmedical words.

I believe that here, rather than at the level of institutional changes, there has been a real impact and a real difference.

MEDITATION 3: JESUS IN THE CARE OF STRANGERS
Mark 15:21–36

It was never the intention of the Gospels to provide medical information about Jesus' death. It is not obvious to most persons today why crucifixion killed; we just assume it did. It is certainly not clear why Jesus' own time on the cross was so short, since normally victims of this torture lived on for several days. As different as his death is in almost all respects from the deaths of patients in modern hospitals who are the focus of the death awareness movement, there is one feature they share with him: they are left in the care of strangers. Except in the Gospel of John, where Jesus is attended by his mother and his favorite disciple, Jesus dies without the presence of friends or followers. Those around him are strangers, and many of them are his enemies.

But not everyone. Several small details in Mark's narrative stand out as instances of caretaking or assistance even in the ghastly environment of public execution. The first is the most ambivalent. "A certain man from Cyrene, Simon, the father of Alexander and Rufus, was passing by on his way in from the country and they forced him to carry the cross" (v. 21). Simon is identified in terms of his home and his family, but his role in the story is as involuntary helper in a public execution of a stranger. Why should Jesus have needed a helper, when it was the common practice to have condemned criminals carry their own crosses out to the place of the skull? This practice must parallel that of having the condemned dig their own graves, then stand beside them to be shot, saving the executioners extra work. Was Jesus already too weak to manage his own cross, hence Simon's forced conscription? Possibly. Even Jesus could not literally obey his own injunction to "pick up your cross"; he depended on the physical strength of another.

The other two instances are of quasi-medical caretaking: "They offered him wine mixed with myrrh" (v. 23) and later, "One man ran, filled a sponge with wine vinegar, put it on a stick, and offered it to Jesus to drink" (v. 36). These are both examples of palliative care, for wine and myrrh would have dulled the pain. In John's Gospel, the second case is palliative in an even simpler sense. This act is in response to Jesus' own plaintive, "I am thirsty" (19:28). In Mark's account, the man who does this actually intervenes with the tormenting crowd: "Now leave him alone. Let's see if Elijah comes to take him down" (v. 36). Instead, Jesus cries out and dies. That some concern for relief of pain and thirst is present among the crowd, even a hostile crowd, is part of the remembered tradition. It is not theologized into a coherent motif of care, for the over-whelming emphasis has been on the guilt of both the Romans and the Jewish leaders in bringing about Jesus' death, extended to the guilt of all humanity who indirectly assisted them. All of us were in some ways responsible for the crucifixion, whatever the legal li-ability of a few. A couple of kind and ineffective deeds by strangers cannot counteract this, the kindly strangers are still in need of redemption, along with all the rest of the world. Never-theless, these acts occurred and are part of the total, tormented pic-ture.

Significantly, Jesus refuses the palliative wine. He does not want to spare himself the pain, or rather, he wants to die with a clear head. No reason is given, but we can imagine that the man who in Gethsemane had assented to the Father's will for him after a struggle, could not allow anything to blur the experience of that will's unfolding. Once he had decided to drink the cup the Father had prepared for him, to drink a cup that dulled his own awareness would have denied the divine purpose. Within this logic, to turn aside from its full bitterness would be to resist the Father's will. To experience "conscious dying" was not in and of itself a prior-ity, but to go through with what God had planned required this.

Without questioning this traditional explanation, we still may supplement it with something else, something more contemporary and close to our own struggle within the medicalization of death. Note the tiny acts of care that occurred at the very last place of Jesus' life. Caretaking is not negated because the wine is refused, and it is not wrong to have offered it; nor are the reed and the sponge going to save his life, any more than Elijah will rescue him. But it is something that even fallen humanity can provide, here at Ground Zero of the atonement. It reminds us that care is a basic response to suffering, and that perhaps care by strangers illustrates this most poignantly.

In this scene, when Jesus' friends, followers, and family are not present, he too must fall back on what hospital patients today learn to depend upon. Behind the scientific aspect of medicine and the medicalization of death lies this capacity to exercise care, and to do so outside the boundaries of families and private emotional bonds. When we hear how hospice returns patients to the "natural" environment of their families, and that home care whenever practical is better than hospital care, we may fall into the trap of equating care with private ties, deep relationships, profound emotional attachments. To some extent, the choice between medicalization in impersonal bureaucratic hospitals and dying as a whole person at home, conflates these two separate factors.

But the care provided by strangers need not be merely professional and efficient; it is, or can be, a true expression of the human capacity to care. This capacity by itself cannot overcome sin and death, cannot even do anything effective for Jesus. But it is there, as an undervalued element in both his passion and in our institutional care for the dying. We should honor it, just as the Gospel authors gave it space.

4

Death as Loss

I.

It is no distortion or exaggeration to say that the newer psychologies of dying are actually psychologies of loss. Indeed, the equation of death with loss is so central to the death awareness movement that it might better be characterized as the recovery of loss, grief, and mourning as basic human realities. This clarifies why so little conflict between the death awareness movement and traditional Christian views and images for death has occurred. In spite of the naturalism of the death awareness movement and its origins in the new ground of medicalized death and hospitals, its overwhelming fascination is with loss as a category. The bulk of its empirical studies actually deal with bereavement, the situation of loss, and mourning. Grief, bereavement, and mourning are not philosophically or theologically opposed to any traditional Christian understandings. I will now show how the pervasive motif of loss occupies a space that permits a kind of integration into Christian spirituality and practice. Very tellingly, Charles Meyer, a Christian chaplain, wrote a book on this subject titled *Surviving Death: A Practical Guide to Caring for the Dying and Bereaved*. What it *now* means to "survive death" is to be plunged into a realm of loss, and it is from this point of view that even Christian writers influenced by the death awareness movement begin.

There are several important claims that constitute a core psychology for the death awareness movement. One of them is that "coming to terms with loss" is a complex psychological process. I put this phrase in quotes to emphasize its role as a cliché or slogan. Loss itself is a fact of life, just as natural as birth and death. But the human drama charted by the death awareness movement is acknowledging and inwardly appropriating the full meanings of the loss. This process is long-term, it requires all our emotional resources, and it is comprehensive. This process is commonly referred to as "grief work." In the title of one book, this assumption is laid bare: *How We Grieve: Relearning the World.*[1] To grieve is an active process of relearning, of ongoing adjustment and accomodation to a world without the lost beloved person or object. There is a myth that this process is simple and intuitively learned; the death awareness movement unanimously disagrees. The effects of grief are long-lasting, and often destructive to the griever and others. A significant proportion of cases require outside, expert interventions.

What inaugurated this picture was not grief in its ordinary, natural setting. This portrayal of coming to terms with loss began with the empirical study of victims of a large-scale disaster, the Coconut Grove fire in a Boston nightclub in 1942. Psychiatrist Erich Lindemann reported his findings of devastation and personal pathology among many of those who survived the fire, and of relatives of those who did not.[2] The survivors had lost loved ones in the disaster, and often felt intense guilt for the fact that *they* had survived while these others had died. Other common reactions (Lindemann's "symptoms" of a "grief syndrome") included preoccupation with the image of the deceased, anger, identification with traits and habits of the deceased, a disruption of basic life patterns, and a wide range of debilitating physical symptoms. "Grief work" emphasizes how difficult and time-consuming the processes of coming to terms with loss are. The bereaved find their continuing symptoms mysterious and distressing. In using medical terms, Lindemann paradoxically pathologizes what he himself clearly believes to be a normal and appropriate response to major loss. The persons who eventually had the most problems were those too numb to begin grief work. They did not experience any of the miserable symptoms, but "blocked off" their grief. Lindemann's medicalization of grief has inhibited and confused what most of the death awareness researchers and clinicians want to communicate: Grief is not, in and of itself, pathological, nor an illness in any sense.

Does it make a difference that the original research on which so much later death awareness movement work is based was done on survivors of a fire, rather than on individuals who lost a relative to illness? Did the nature of the disaster itself—large-scale, sudden, preventable—substantially affect the findings? The answer to this question is both yes and no. Yes, because it now seems as if certain kinds of situations regularly make mourning very, very difficult. "Complicated mourning," to use the most recent, nonpathologizing phrase, is linked to about seven different factors, and a sudden preventable death is itself one of these. Even one death in a preventable fire would give rise to more symptoms than would a loss experienced under less dramatic and traumatic circumstances. A large-scale fire, many of whose survivors were themselves often badly burned, adds to the horror. At one level, then, this atypical situation makes one question why Lindemann's study became so critical for others who investigated mourning, grief work, and bereavement.

The answer is in the chronology. Lindemann's research was published in 1944, and it was not until the late 1960s and early 1970s that what I have been calling the "death awareness movement" began as an identifiable force. Lindemann's work was then rediscovered, with minimal interest in how the specific research situation could have biased an understanding of bereavement in general. What had not been of widespread, general interest in 1944 became very relevant and central to many psychological writers and practitioners by the early 1970s. The original uniqueness of the situation kept it from being important at the time, except as an interesting study of the psychology of disaster. The same research became very important a generation later when it became a study, not of a traumatic disaster, but of coming to terms with loss for everyone. Americans were ready to hear about loss, bereavement, and grief work in the 1970s, but we were not yet in 1944.

Why did grief remain an unnoticed, undeveloped topic for so long, and why, when it was "discovered," was it discovered by means of a study of traumatic large-scale disaster victims and survivors? One reason is that in a cultural atmosphere where death had become "wild," bereavement too, and indeed any response to death, also became unmentioned, avoided, and silenced. "How I mourned a death" is not a subject for autobiographies from the 1940s through the 1960s, a period that brought us few accounts of an individual's dying.

"Wild death" by itself is not an explanation, however, Why did bereavement go so out of view, out of style, as an experience? A different level of speculation looks at the national situations of 1944 and the early 1970s and notes that two wars were fought at those times, both far away from home, but with very different impacts on the nation. In 1944, when Lindemann's "acute grief syndrome" was proposed to explain the problems in living faced by the fire survivors and their families, America was involved in a war that was *believed in,* and was also by that time felt to be winnable. The deaths most in the news were the deaths of soldiers, deaths that were given public and heroic meanings. For the families of the dead, there may have been as many private problems as Lindemann or later researchers could imagine, but for the public, grief was speakable, it was part of the tale of sacrifice to avenge Pearl Harbor or to fight the evils of Nazism and Fascism. Civilians during that war shared a sense of purpose, of participating in an intense, important collective effort. Yes, there were some exceptions; for some groups the story was more complicated, and indeed very bitter (the Japanese Americans interned in Wyoming are an obvious example). However, my parents volunteered at the local police station and watched for enemy planes flying over Manhattan. Others took the wheels off the family car and used the themes of sacrifice and patriotism to validate this gas saving.

By the early 1970s, another war was underway, with vastly different public attitudes toward its deaths. For those who supported the war in Vietnam, it was a patriotic duty to serve in the military if drafted, and to do nothing that would show disrespect for the men who were fighting. But very little enthusiasm for the cause itself could be generated; there was no Pearl Harbor to avenge. For those who opposed the war, the deaths of Americans were a tragic waste, and the horrendous number of civilian deaths were cruel and preventable. Thus, no one's deaths could be given an unambiguous heroic public meaning. Recall how for Kübler-Ross war itself is based on denial of death, as we project our fear of death onto an enemy and try to destroy it through mass killing.[3] From this point of view, the deaths of soldiers can never contribute to a genuine understanding of death as a natural and acceptable part of life, nor can the heroic ideal of sacrifice mean anything. The absence of this motif in the experiences of dying hospital patients is only one aspect of its absence overall in the death awareness movement's imagery.

In the post-Vietnam ethos of the death awareness movement's flowering, antipathy to heroic models ran very high. Medicine had appropriated military imagery, and the ideal of "conquering" death and disease made the dying patient a medical failure. But this antipathy was also based on revulsion against a war that was fought in the absence of compelling moral meanings. What remained in the wake of that war was grief, shattered lives of Vietnam veterans, and an inability to come to terms with what happened. Under these conditions, private grief became a topic, became visible, became recoverable in a way that it had not in 1944. So Lindemann's study of survivors of a massive, tragic, and preventable disaster became a road map for how to chart grief and grief work. What made Lindemann's essay so powerful and appealing in the early 1970s was that the Vietnam War itself was just such a disaster, as senseless and destructive as the nightclub fire, as impossible to find meaningful. Public silence about the war during the 1970s went hand in hand with the growth of attention to grief, bereavement, and mourning as private, personal responses to loss.

This is a speculative explanation. Americans died of many causes during the Vietnam era, and private grief was an ongoing reality in both wars. Even after the Vietnam Memorial in Washington D.C. was constructed to officially acknowledge and mourn the dead, an interest in bereavement and grief continues as central in the death awareness movement. What I suggest is that naming death as loss, and concentrating on mourning as personal coming to terms with loss, is linked not to the absolute presence or absence of bereavement, but to the relative presence or absence of culturally sanctioned public meanings for death. Such public meanings might overshadow or compete with loss. When the public meanings vanished in the case of the Vietnam War, the experience left a widespread interest in loss and mourning, which the death awareness movement built upon.

However, this explanation assumes that the Vietnam War was impossible to find meaningful. No civilians made sacrifices of their time and energy to help further the cause of keeping the Diem regime in power. But this is both hindsight and a naive view of wars as making sense in and of themselves, or failing to do so. A less naive view assumes that mobilization for a meaningful war is a human activity, and sustaining a war's meaning is also a human activity. Why did this human activity fail in the late 1960s and 1970s, when it had succeeded in the early 1940s?

The pre-Vietnam ethos was already filled with attention to inner experience, to psychological growth and self-actualization, even if the psychologies of the human potential movement flourished more fully in the post-Vietnam ethos. Attention to the humanistic and private dimensions of experience characterized the alienated students of the 1960s. These qualities preceded specific political causes and situations. The Harvard students of Kenneth Keniston's study *The Uncommitted* (1960) shared inward psychological fragility that left them vulnerable to experiences of loss, emptiness, and separation.[4] These persons may not have been typical American youth, but they were an interesting elite whose inner world resonated with some of the motifs of the death awareness movement as it developed a decade later. Did Keniston's alienated students mature into the first generation of death awareness researchers and clinicians? Even more likely, did their pervasive awareness of the dangers of attachments, and their anxieties over inward emptiness, help them validate bereavement as a process of coming to terms with loss? They were already in a state of loss when Keniston studied them; not the loss by death of a loved person, but more a loss of the capacity to feel, relate, and commit themselves emotionally. The loss and emptiness of the uncommitted and their cohorts was present before the Vietnam War, and before the death awareness movement identified coming to terms with loss as a significant element in human life. In the aftermath, the post-Vietnam ethos, this preexisting sense of loss was given a voice in the death awareness movement. In the shadow of this ethos, what the death awareness movement does with loss is central to our discussion.

II.

I have used Lindemann's phrase "grief work," which is actually taken from Freud's essay on "Mourning and Melancholia" as the technical equivalent for the colloquial expression, "coming to terms with loss." Grief work is "relearning the world," an attempt to restore and finally relinquish the lost beloved within one's psyche. It is also a struggle to rebuild one's daily life, one's other relationships, one's sense of self and future. All of this takes time, and since the early 1970s researchers have been concerned with both the best way to conceptualize the processes, and to accurately estimate the time they take to complete. A subordinate theme is to distinguish pathological from normal mourning, a task that is impossible so long as the real parameters of normal mourning remain undefined. There is increasing awareness of how complex grief work is, how long it really takes, and how so much in our society impedes its successful completion. Unlike many of the other issues tackled by the death awareness movement, such as whether death is natural and what this means, these questions about mourning can be empirically researched. Granted, the distinction between normal and pathological always requires value judgments as well as facts, but at least one can study large numbers of widows from the time of bereavement through to five or ten years afterward to discover which factors make for difficult mourning. (Widows are most frequently studied because there are plenty of them, and they are likely to be older, less peripatetic, and so easier to follow up on than other populations of the bereaved.) The philosophical questions come in trying to conceptualize the process, for each approach accepts certain key cultural biases about human functioning and how our identities develop over time.

The earlier research took its cue from Lindemann himself. Mourning, the work of grief, occurs in stages. There is the "acute grief" stage, often marked by physical symptoms and psychic numbness. Then a second and much more extended period of misery follows, when anger, guilt, preoccupation with the dead person, and social isolation are all common feelings and behaviors. Finally, grief recedes, and new patterns of functioning can be mastered. The person is then "over it," and can get on with life and form new attachments. This goal is the unquestioned and unequivocable desire of all who deal with the bereaved, and indeed of all groups in American society today. No religious groups forbid the remarriage of widows and widowers, although children may resist new stepparents, at least for a time. All the examples of the perpetual mourners from the past, such as Queen Victoria, become today's negative examples.

Lindemann believed that a year for grief work was about normal. The problems he identified, the situations of pathological mourning, began when the onset of grief work was blocked or delayed. Those who did not start, or started late, never finished. So overwhelming was the loss that they could not even try to come to terms with it. Or, in some cases, the practical responsibilities of care for others (such as young children) were so daunting and exhausting that they postponed their own grief work indefinitely.

This stages model also guided the initial work of Colin Parkes, a major contributor to the empirical research on grief and loss in adults. Parkes constructs the grief work as a search on the part of the bereaved to find the lost beloved.[5] This search includes such common symptoms of mourning as intense, vivid remembering of the lost person—attempts to restore that person as an intrapsychic reality. It also helps account for the frequent reports by the bereaved that they sensed the presence of the dead person nearby. This too is construed as an attempt to restore what had been lost, not as a pathological hallucination (and not as an actual visit from a dead spirit either!). Quick remarriages after a spouse's death are also attempts to restore the dead, in the shape of a new person. Marriages made under these conditions will quickly turn wretched, as the new spouse refuses to be a replacement, and the lost beloved is still lost. It takes a long time before the search is really abandoned, when accomodation to the irrevocable loss finally occurs. In fact, the tone of Parkes's research is to caution our society in its urgency to see people "get over it" and "get on with their lives." Mourning is a longer and more enervating process than we imagine. For a substantial proportion of the bereaved, it never really is accomplished. Difficult, pathological, complicated: the terms vary, but some people become stuck in mourning and never complete the process. These are not necessarily blocked grievers. They may very early in their bereavement experience uncontrollable and devastating anxiety. Perhaps this particular death was only their most recent in a whole series of unmanageable losses.

A further development in the study of mourning was to let go of the notion of stages, and to conceptualize the grief work as "tasks." William Worden's formulation of "The Four Tasks of Mourning" in 1982 became standard for counselors and therapists. This terminology puts the emphasis on work, activity, the initiative of the mourner to do something, rather than to let stages simply happen. The four tasks are:

1. To accept the reality of the loss.
2. To experience the pain of grief.
3. To adjust to an environment in which the deceased is missing.
4. To withdraw emotional energy and reinvest it in another relationship.[6]

A work ethic is obviously alive and well in psychological discourse, as these complex human situations are labelled "tasks" and clinicians promote an activist stance toward their completion. However, the real impact of this is to make researchers very cautious about a time frame. Worden declares, "In my view, mourning is finished when the tasks of mourning are accomplished."[7] There should be no other answer to the question, "How long does mourning last?" This preserves the bereaved from unwarranted pressure to move through stages quickly, or to meet expectations that within a year they will be "over it." The concern is that society considerably underestimates the difficulty and complexity of mourning, and does not recognize that mourning is hard work. Perhaps in a society where work alone is considered productive activity, it is necessary to emphasize this point over and over. Especially because one common result of bereavement will be a loss of ordinary productivity on the job or a drop in grades at school, this model highlights the fact that the bereaved is doing some work of his or her own that cannot be avoided.

Although "tasks" language overcomes some problems, the project of conceptualizing grief and the process of coming to terms with loss continues. By the early 1990s, "tasks" seemed unconvincing. Attig lists the above four demands, and then states categorically, "They are simply not tasks at all. Tasks, as I understand them and the dictionary defines them, are circumscribable, modest in scale, and completable. This is not true for any of the items [Worden] lists."[8] These items label various facets—emotional, behavioral, social—of the coping process. As "relearning the world," what happens in grieving transcends any model of tasks. Moreover, when looked at as a comprehensive coping with loss, time frame becomes irrelevant. One may speak of an ongoing lifelong process of reaching accommodations. At each new place in life, one revisits and reaccommodates to the loss. Attig and others allow that this entire process does not proceed at the same intensity throughout, but it is a mistake to assume that mourning is ever completed.

A further step along this route is taken in Therese Rando's monumental *Treatment of Complicated Mourning*. Rando discards "tasks" in favor of what she calls "the six 'R' processes of mourning":

1. Recognize the loss.
2. React to the separation.
3. Recollect and reexperience the deceased and the relationship.
4. Relinquish the old attachments to the deceased and the old assumptive world.
5. Readjust to move adaptively into the new world without forgetting the old.
6. Reinvest.[9]

Here the controlling framework becomes psychological processes that need not occur in any set sequence, that in fact are simultaneous and overlapping, and that end only at the griever's own death. "Recognize the loss" is aimed against denial, and consistent denial prevents any adequate effort to meet the challenge of the other processes. But note how complex each of these R-processes is. "Recollect and reexperience the deceased and the relationship" is a necessary part of what the bereaved must do, but if the relationship was long and complicated, this process can be endlessly redone, so that new aspects of the old relationship must come to the fore and be reexperienced even after the dominant aspects have been both recollected and relinquished. A death that occurs in one's childhood will have one set of meanings and implications at the time, but will need to be partially "re-grieved" when the person becomes an adult, when he or she takes on the role of being someone else's parent, when other deaths occur that evoke again the memories of the lost childhood relationship.

Note also how Rando's formulation carefully avoids a model of abandoned search, of "getting over it," of simple move from past to future. We human beings are our pasts and our relationships. It is not appropriate to lose or forget or block out someone from our memories just because that person has died. A relationship with the dead person persists, even if its terms are vastly different now that he or she is dead. This is an important clue to why mourning appears so difficult to conceptualize, even for therapists committed to taking it seriously and working with the bereaved. There is a wide-spread bias toward a model of old-to-new, toward tasks accomplished then forgotten, and perhaps toward the old immigrant myth of the "fresh start," the new identity that lets the old one vanish in the "melting pot" of America. The search model uses the idea of a literal search and replace to conceptualize the ongoing presence of the dead within the lives of the living. Rando's R-processes imagery lets the dead exist differently, but they are certainly still part of who we are. In the paradoxical words of Simone Weil, "The absence of the dead is their way of appearing." They do indeed retain a mode of appearing even when literally gone, and Rando helps understand this much better than earlier theorists.

The more long-term and complex mourning's six R-processes become, the harder to determine what the boundaries between ordinary and pathological mourning are. Rando prefers the nonmedical label of "complicated mourning," although one of the predisposing factors for the latter is a history of major mental illness. Others include the mode of death (e.g., traumatic, preventable), lack of perceived social support, and the history of the relationship with the deceased. It now seems that early, long-term personal patterns of attachment predispose some persons to complicated, difficult mourning. Clinicians should both discover who is at risk for complicated, protracted mourning and how to identify such persons early in bereavement. Trouble at school, work-related problems, and disruptions of other relationships are often traced back to mourning, and there are tales of obvious complicated mourning misdiagnosed as something else.[10]

The therapeutic solution to complicated mourning is to transform it into simple or ordinary mourning. This seems obvious; "mourning" is an absolutely necessary and intrinsic part of living. But this, of course, is what many "complicated mourners" resist most. Breaking the whole experience into six R-processes does help the therapist decide which aspects of mourning to push first with particular clients. It calls for judgment about whether the problem is denial that the death is real or whether it is inability to reinvest. But the goal remains for all clients to transform complicated into ordinary mourning. This is not a glamorous goal. It is parallel, in fact, to Freud's statement to a prospective patient, as quoted by Philip Rieff: "You will be able to convince yourself that much will be gained if we succeed in transforming your hysterical misery into common unhappiness."[11] Common unhappiness and simple mourning are not the kind of goals that in and of themselves can generate much enthusiasm. There may indeed be "good grief," but it is still not much fun, especially given what Rando and Parkes and others have learned about the messy and time-consuming nature of even ordinary mourning.

An ominous and alarming note sounds in some of this literature on mourning and loss. The instances of complicated mourning seem to be increasing in our society. More and more people are less capable of moving into the work of grief. For others, complicated mourning is further worsened due to addictions, depression, or other problems. There are more cases where frayed relationships and broken long-term ties take their toll on the bereaved; fragile and insecure attachments do not lead to less, but to *more* emotional turmoil when ruptured by death. There seem to be fewer secure sources of support to assist the bereaved.

An additional problem is now known as disenfranchised grief, from the book of that name edited by Kenneth Doka.[12] Disenfranchised grief is grief denied legitimacy by society, by the family, or by the mourner himself. This problem ranges from situations where the relationship itself is condemned, as with the death of a gay lover, to where the griever is considered incapable of really feeling the loss, as with the mentally handicapped. The disenfranchised griever must do his grief work in secret, and so automatically suffers from one of the conditions found to be key predictors of complicated mourning: perceived lack of social support. (Note that it is "perceived" rather than actual support that is missing; I speak of the griever's perspective, which may not match what a sociologist would see.) Disenfranchised grief, defined in this fashion, has probably always been present in human societies. Adulterous lovers probably always mourned in secret, children's grief for dead siblings was probably not taken too seriously by adults, and those who survived massacres or conquests were expected to be grateful, not publicly grief-stricken. Nevertheless, in a society where the rules for relationships have changed rapidly, and where often the problem is that no one knows the rules, the occasions for disenfranchised grief multiply.

To summarize the picture painted by this empirical and clinical research on mourning, coming to terms with loss is complex, comprehensive, ongoing, and very, very difficult for most persons. For some, it is impossible to do this adequately; they become perpetual mourners, their lives spoiled and wretched, and undoubtedly they make the lives of those around them more unhappy too. Unlike death, which happens at the end of our lives, loss happens all through them. To imagine an identity without the experience of loss is to make the same mistake Ivan Ilych's colleagues make: Loss is not something external to one's self, it does not happen just to others. To accept this view of loss is to engage the death awareness movement at a different level than debate over whether death is natural. It is to break through certain emphases of American society, on the future rather than the past, on life as a series of stages or tasks that one can accomplish quickly and in sequence. The message is that sad experiences, and how we handle these, count in who we are. These sad experiences should be noticed and given psychological space and support. Behind the unromantic language of R-processes there is a compelling vision of life as often overwhelming, where indeed the race is not always to the swift, where real growth requires getting deeper into sorrow and the past than floating on one's own heights and hopes. The "re" prefix of all the R-processes carries this weight.

III.

In all the literature on bereavement, mourning, and grief, there is never any doubt that the person or object lost is *other* than the self. Attachment, separation, search, remembering the relationship—all these ideas make sense if there are two persons involved or a lost object that in some way takes on the status of another person (e.g., a pet). So obvious is this that it ought to seem odd to apply ideas of grief work to the anticipation of the self's own death. Yet it is possible that

Kübler-Ross derived her whole framework, the scheme of five stages of dying from Lindemann's work. These stages of denial, anger, bargaining, depression (subdivided into reactive and preparatory), and acceptance became the favorite ideal for several decades of thinking and practical care, even as almost everyone agreed that the stages did not appear in sequence, and that the model worked as a moral ideal more than as a psychological description. Every dying person, it was hoped, could reach acceptance before death; patients should move through denial and anger. No matter how often and insistently Kübler-Ross and others familiar with the model claimed their purpose was to meet each dying person where that person was—emotionally, socially, spiritually—the sequential structure encouraged the aim of moving through the stages as quickly as possible.

This model rests on a presumed parallel with the process of mourning. There is a gradual, orderly process of recognizing the anticipated end of one's life, recollecting and reexperiencing the important relationships and ties of that life, and relinquishing one's attachment to it. These R-processes seem to correspond closely to the denial, reactive depression, and acceptance stages of Kübler-Ross's scheme. Indeed, when Kübler-Ross proposed her scheme, she seemed happy to see it applied to the soon-to-be-bereaved families, so that their anticipatory grief parallels the stages of the dying person herself.

Yet by now the multiple problems with this assumed parallel should be obvious. The death of the self is simply not the same as the death of another. "Search," in Parkes' sense of an intense urge to re-find the missing person, is an alleged biologically based adaptive behavior aimed at maximizing the survival of a temporarily isolated young primate. That is its origin in our remote protohuman past. Search in this sense cannot be applied to oneself. The struggle for identity in the face of impending death cannot be modelled on this behavior pattern. Notice how different the possible meaning and application of this term might be in the two situations, and the whole parallel becomes filled with dubious equivalences.

Another obvious misfit between the death of another and the impending death of oneself is the role of denial in the two situations.

Denial in the context of one's own anticipated death is found universally, although it is rarely total. It is exemplified by statements such as, "When I get out of the hospital . . . I'm only a bit run-down . . . They mixed my X-rays up with someone else's . . . " A frantic search for miracle cures, refusal to follow dietary restrictions, and false claims of physical improvement are considered behavioral signs of denial. (These examples come right out of the Kübler-Ross discussion, and can be multiplied by the hundred.) Denial can be on again, off again ("fluctuating") and selective (maintained with one person, but abandoned with others). Denial not only shields the self, but has an adaptive function in maintaining relationships that would end without it. Defined this broadly, it certainly seems to be present in virtually all dying persons to some extent. By contrast, true denial in the context of bereavement is rarely the problem. When Rando lists "Recognize the loss" as the first R-process, she does not imply that many people flatly refuse to accept that a loss has occurred. They do not pretend that the person who has died is still alive; they plan funerals, they behave realistically on the surface. They may need to recognize the loss at the deeper emotional levels that clinicians find important, but it is a rare case of bereavement where denial is truly the pervasive problem as it is among the dying.

A third difference between the two situations is how time works in each. Recall that Lindemann originally thought that a year was sufficient to complete grief work. Many dying persons have at least this much forewarning of their deaths, and so clinicians imagined a parallel of intense anticipated grief work for oneself, lasting a finite period of time. Within this picture, sudden death is a problem insofar as no anticipation on anyone's part will have occurred. The dying person will have avoided the whole process, and the family will be unprepared, will not have experienced any anticipatory grief.

However, as we have seen, the notion of a set time frame for mourning is now believed to be misleading and unhelpful. Mourning in the sense Attig and Rando understand it is a lifelong accomodation to loss. If so, no parallel with the situation of the dying can be relied upon. Or rather, specific factors in the prognosis, the progression of the illness, and its medical treatment need to be acknowledged as directly relevant to the scheme of coming to terms with death, as they were not in the original Kübler-Ross model. In the case of illnesses known to be fatal but where a very long period of time is given between the initial prognosis and the time of death, there will be too much time to devote entirely to the psychological tasks of the R-processes. For instance, cystic fibrosis has its own trajectory, as anthropologist Myra Blueblood-Langer's study of afflicted children and families shows.[13] After the initial diagnosis, some of the processes of coping with impending loss were experienced, but the families then focused on daily living and care for the sick child, and adapted to a steady situation medically by bracketing off all concern with the eventual anticipated death. Only when the illness started to assert itself dramatically and catastrophically did the children's and families' attention turn back to impending death. The changed experience of living with AIDS is an even clearer case of how a model of constant anticipation of one's own death shifts to an assumed period of relative health prior to the final onset of a cascade of illnesses. Once these aspects of dying, particularized to the individual illnesses and disease processes, are noticed, the weakness of the parallel between death of the other and anticipated death of self is plain.

Yet surely there are some similarities, some truly parallel features of the two situations? The parallel assumes that both call on the self's resources for coping with massive threat and disruption. The mourner and the one who is dying must struggle to "relearn the world" and question their own assumptions about it. They must reflect on the meanings of the past and attempt to form a life story that will ring true. In this, the parallel still makes some intuitive sense. Much of what Kübler-Ross discussed under the category of "reactive depression" (unfinished emotional business) corresponds to the third and fourth R-processes (recollect and reexperience, relinquish).[14] If so, then to speak of a life review is more appropriate than a global label such as "depression," which is easy to confuse with the psychiatric condition. Do all dying persons engage in this?

Not exactly, but the parallel works when it is confined to R-processes that focus on reviewing and reassessing the past, rather than on any other dimensions of the situations.

These specific processes are the fundamental material for stories of anticipated death. The protagonist must struggle with recollecting, reexperiencing, and relinquishing the past, just as Ivan Ilych did. Normally this yields more sense of the past's inner worth, its secret treasures, its living heritage. Stewart Alsop's autobiography, *Stay of Execution,* starts as he is sick from a blood disease. He recollects his life as a journalist, a father, and finally as a soldier who escaped wartime death in France. All the while he knows he will not escape this time and will soon die.[15] This focus on questioning, recollecting, and reexperiencing the past and its relationships is what the situations of anticipating one's own death and mourning that of another seem to share.

Beyond this the parallel fails completely. Recall how the thrust of all contemporary studies of mourning as a process assume that its ultimate outcome is to reinvest, to return to a new life. "To move adaptively into the new world" — Rando's fifth R-process — is a sensible goal insofar as there is a "new world" out there for the bereaved. Even when stages of mourning are discarded, the processes of grief work presuppose recovery as a desirable consummation. In the case of the dying, acceptance and relinquishing attachments to life are the aim. Death is an ending, insofar as it is a natural event as the death awareness movement advocates. Whether one is fully alive right up until the moment of death, as the hospice philosophy insists, or whether the dying moves into a borderland where special states of consciousness and unusual experiences are normal, there are no equivalents to Rando's fifth and sixth R-processes (readjust and reinvest) for the dying. In this sense, dying is loss and purely loss.

But is one's own death "loss"? Is it only an ending? The model I examine focuses attention exclusively on this, while insisting that such a loss is appropriate, ultimately acceptable. One of the ironies of Kübler-Ross's initial presentation of acceptance is that her example of an accepting patient, the pious dentist Dr. G., holds a

thoroughly different view of what his death means: "I do look forward to meeting the Lord, but at the same time I would like to stay
around on earth as long as possible. The thing I feel most deeply
is the parting of the family."[16] This is clearly not the same as pure
letting go or loss, although separation is indeed an aspect of dying.
The more traditional understanding held by Dr. G. treats death as
a transition, a process of letting go but also anticipating what lies
ahead. Bunyan's pilgrims could not have used a loss model at all,
for however dangerous the river crossing might be, on the other
side lay their long-anticipated destination, the Celestial City. They
will, one assumes, readjust to move adaptively into that world and
be eager to forget the old world through which they have travelled
so painfully. They have already reinvested their energies into that
future by leaving home in the first place.

Thus, Rando's fifth and sixth R-processes cannot truly be made
to fit into a model of dying. To the best of my knowledge, no one
among contemporary spiritual writers has tried to construct such
connections between the "readjust" and "reinvest" of mourning,
and transition to a transcendent, eternal existence after this life. In
the contemporary literature of the death awareness movement,
there is an openness to spirituality, but not—in the psychological
literature—a thorough and theoretically grounded renunciation of
the loss model as a way to image death. Indeed, even to imagine
taking R-processes 5 and 6 and applying them to preparation for a
life everlasting seems thoroughly bizarre, well outside the range of
possibilities available through the death awareness movement.
The appropriation of the death awareness movement's language
and imagery by Christians has not taken this pathway.

Let us return to the difference between the death of the other, for
which mourning is the appropriate response, and the death of the
self. Death as loss directly fits the former, and the best of the contemporary empirical research confines itself to this situation. There
are many more problems assimilating the death of the self into a
model of grief work. Even with the image of loss, the parallel is
strained. Without stages, what remains are some parallels in regard
to the third and fourth R-processes (recollect and reexperience,

relinquish). The experience of denial in the dying does not parallel the first two R-processes, but is far more pervasive. Finally, there is the overall aim inherent in all contemporary studies of bereavement: the assumption that the goal is to move into new relationships, new ties within the world. This is a goal that cannot apply to the dying, unless one moves outside the model of loss and dying as natural. Important and obvious as these differences are, in the last thirty years it has been common to conflate the two situations. If loss is the major contribution of the death awareness movement, it can well address the experience of mourning, but flounder in comprehending the experience of dying. Recognize this, and the exact shape of the death awareness movement and its interactions with Christian faith will become clearer.

IV.

For most of Christian history the focus on one's own death was balanced by a collective emphasis on the day of Christ, the last judgment, and the general resurrection. When the dying and death of each unique individual became central in the late Middle Ages, the *Ars Moriendi* provided guidance and a rich set of images to help the dying person understand death as a transition out of life and into direct encounter with God. Meanwhile, the family was left on the outside of this drama. The anxieties, griefs, and ruptured lives of family members were irrelevant. After the death they were in a situation of bereavement, but it receives no theological attention whatsoever. Even the practices of saying masses and prayers for the deceased in Purgatory, which we might see as a means for the living to remain linked with the deceased, were promoted for the benefit of the dead and not for the spiritual benefit of the bereaved. It is no exaggeration to say that mourning as a special, marked off spiritual situation has never been of interest or importance to Christian doctrine. Mourning practices, however seriously observed, seem to have been sanctioned by the church, but without any of the elaboration given to doctrines of eternal life or the destinations of the dead.

To use Ariès's categories, "the death of the self" far outweighs "the death of the other" in the focus of traditional Christian reflection and practices. By contrast, the death as loss imagery discerned and elaborated in the death awareness movement takes the latter experience as central, and only by extension (with all the problems we have just examined) applies this back to the death of the self. This creates a situation of potential conflict but also actual contemporary complementarity. Christian faith covers the destiny of the deceased, both immediately before and immediately after death, while the psychological focus of the death awareness movement can take up the slack, begin with the situation of the bereaved, and concentrate upon their experience as loss, as R-processes or "relearning the world." To a great extent, pastoral counseling literature focused on bereavement does indeed seem to accept and work within this split, appropriating the death awareness movement to fill a niche left bare by traditional concerns. It is not, I must insist, that one set of concerns is innately "spiritual" while the second is "merely psychological." Indeed, the death awareness movement contains and conveys its own spirituality, its own ultimate concerns and images to express these. Therefore, a truce or division of labor, or even helpful complementarity, eventually creates new patterns of meaning that refuse to remain separated from each other.

To make this discussion far more concrete, turn to the recent debates over the meanings and purposes of Christian funerals. What should a funeral do? For whose benefit is a funeral? Note that all funerals occur very soon after the death. From the perspective of mourners, the benefits of the funeral will be restricted by this time factor. Unlike the rites in Japanese Buddhism, which continue for periods up to thirty-three years after the death, the funeral in Christian tradition is a onetime event.

By far the most significant thing to say about traditional funerals is that, liturgically, they are focused on the transition from this life into something else, a transition that the dead person has experienced, but that needs to be proclaimed to all who remain alive. In words from the older form of Rite I of the Burial from *The Book of Common Prayer* of the Episcopal Church:

We are mortal, formed of the earth, and unto earth shall we return. For so thou didst ordain when thou createdst me, saying, "Dust thou art, and unto dust shall thou return." All we go down to the dust; yet even at the grave we make our song: Alleluia, alleluia, alleluia.[17]

In this passage, the funeral is both for the dead and the living: the dead who will be ritually acknowledged as returned to dust, and the living who will be called on to remember that we will join them soon. The "we" of the liturgy here is not the family qua family, but "me," the existentially alone individual whose relation to God is what matters most.

One can see how a traditional funeral might function as a call to remember one's own need for divine mercy and salvation. The overwhelming stress on "we" as sharing the mortality of all creatures, on our need for "holiness and righteousness . . . pardon and peace"[18] in the face of our own inevitable deaths, makes the funeral a time for return and repentance, for seeking one's own relationship with God. Insofar as prayers in the Burial rite of *The Book of Common Prayer* refer directly to the needs and conditions of the living, this is their focus. Rite I is the more old fashioned and traditional service, which expresses in more stark and unmitigated fashion the emphasis on death, mortality, and the presence of God as the creator of all that go down to the dust. Comfort for the bereaved is a very minor theme; only two optional petitions mention it.[19]

Christian funerals moved in two different directions, one informed by theology and the other by pastoral care. The text for Rite II, the revised Burial service, reveals the influence of both. The theological emphasis shifts to stress on the resurrection, on Christian hope, on the victory of Jesus Christ over death, on eschatology as outweighing mortality. This theological shift was legitimated by scholarly study of the New Testament, where the day of Christ and the kingdom of God surpass the focus on death, ending, and destruction. The Christian gospel is not a message about death, but about victory over death; not about "going down to the dust," but about being raised to glory. For theologians, this is not denial of death, but an authentic recovery of the fullness of the gospel.

This message stresses Christian faith as hopeful and focused on God's ultimate Yes to creation and humanity—or so its proponents argued. So influential were they that funeral rites in many Christian denominations were revised to reflect these concerns.

Ironically, the pastoral care perspective, assimilating the death awareness movement's attention to death as loss for the survivors, wanted a different message at the funeral. The new message of hope was worse than the old. In a Rite I style of funeral liturgy, all had focused on mortality, to share in the death of the one who had already gone down to the dust. Although the mourners were not given explicit attention as mourners, the overall somberness and sadness of the occasion was honored. There was no reason to dispute a basic realism in the face of death, no way to doubt that a death had occurred. A more positive, upbeat, and hopeful funeral liturgy does potentially raise doubt as to how well anyone recognizes the reality of death. For the mourners, at the very time when they were struggling to acknowledge the death and begin to cope with overwhelming sadness, the liturgies asked them to rejoice. Emphasis on hope, victory, and resurrection seem, perhaps especially in the context of American life, to be saying that even a sad event wasn't really sad. Was it actually wrong for Christians to mourn or to feel a sense of loss at all? For in this theological stress on promise and resurrection, the church seemed to conspire with American society as a whole to deny both death and a space for grief. In the words of Kenneth Mitchell and Herbert Anderson, "The theological assertion is accurate, but from a pastoral perspective the theological priority has been misplaced."[20] The dead person may indeed be on track for the resurrection, but if so, those who survive still face a real loss. Curiously, the separation between dead and living is now much more obvious than in the "we" language of the older rites.

Rite II in *The Book of Common Prayer* explicitly includes the loss model and its imagery into a rite nevertheless still focused on the destiny of the dead. References to the bereaved as in special need of comfort are now expanded. These are modest additions, but directly aimed at the mourning family and friends.

Lord, you consoled Martha and Mary in their distress; draw near to us who mourn for *N.,* and dry the tears of those who weep.

You wept at the grave of Lazarus, your friend; comfort us in our sorrow . . .

Comfort us in our sorrows at the death of our brother (sister); let our faith be our consolation, and eternal life our hope.[21]

Note how explicitly the weeping of Jesus is evoked at the time of his friend's death. It is permissible to show grief; it is not a sign of lack of faith. Although it might be argued that Jesus wept over the lack of faith of those around him (John 11:33–35), this is not the meaning of the behavior preserved here. Jesus felt sorrow, for death is and remains a sad occasion, even when raising of the dead is part of the total picture. Mourning is not shameful. *The Book of Common Prayer* does not stress that death is a loss, but at least now leaves room for this idea. The obvious impact of criticism from pastoral caregivers sympathetic to the death awareness movement is to complement the theology of resurrection with knowledge that death is a loss. It must be dealt with as a loss by those who survive.

How much consolation, comfort, and understanding these texts actually bring is not the point. The only Christian rites come so soon after the death that the extended and complex process of mourning is barely underway at the time when these prayers are said. Nevertheless, it seems that here death as a loss for those who remain alive is a significant reality, a meaning that can find some place within the Christian landscape of faith. It may never be the central meaning of death, but it can coexist with earlier meanings even in these most formal, official rites. Equally apparent is the lack of anything after burial to address the spiritual concerns of the bereaved. From the perspective of the loss model and the death awareness movement's focus on this, it is a sad gap in our ways to grapple with death that there is no rite for anything later on, for the whole complex process of mourning that may last months, a year, or one's entire life. Unlike the aforementioned Buddhist funeral rites, which give the family something ritual to do days, months, and years later, Christians' official and public practices seem, from this perspective, incredibly truncated and insufficient.

In the past, culture rather than church gave mourning a structure. There did not need to be extra rites for mourners in the prayer book because they were surrounded and guided by a multitude of restrictions, prohibitions, and set patterns to follow that derived from their societies. Women wore black and did not go to parties or dance. Men wore black armbands. Between the public social structuring of mourning and the day-to-day survival issues, the private grief of individuals existed, but without religious attention to it at the same official level as a funeral. Now, however, when the public role of mourner has vanished and the practical problems have been somewhat alleviated (we no longer hear of fathers who place their children in orphanages because no wife is available to cook and care for the children), some note the religious gap and sadly ponder it. What does it say that there is no ritual attention to mourning as a special spiritual state in Christianity?

Here is a place where the death awareness movement locates itself outside any one religious tradition, but adjacent to several. As a secular movement with roots in psychology, it is free to impact upon religious groups via their members' sensibilities and experiences, as in the inclusion of pastoral concern for mourners in the newer Episcopal rite. The death awareness movement has simultaneously worked to sensitize Jews to the strengths of their own practices, particularly the traditional rites of mourning. Unlike Christianity, where theological affirmations have always been given a kind of official priority, Judaism is primarily a tradition of sacred law and practice, which permits an explicit focus on mourning at an official level unknown in Christianity. The rabbinic sages whose interpretations of Torah appear in the Talmud laid down authoritative accounts of how to mourn as a Jew. Rabbinic Judaism requires that all Jews everywhere follow the Halakhah (legal regulations) of mourning. Although the specific practices may be duplicated by Christians in the Near East, they are in the Jewish tradition given an official status, ultimately derived from the Hebrew Bible.

Without a doubt, the impact of the death awareness movement's focus on loss and mourning upon American Jewish understandings of this tradition has been immense. The rabbis may or may not have been expert practical psychologists, but Jewish mourning practices have been defended and validated by the pervasive reliance on death awareness movement ideas.[22] Although today many Jewish families shorten shiva from seven days to three, or postpone the funeral until those living far away can attend, that there is a traditional way to mourn is widely acknowledged. The psychological validation of the mourning period endorses its overall structuredness and its inclusion of feelings such as disruption, depression, guilt, and even anger. This special state meets the needs of the bereaved, is honored by the tradition, and the important emphasis on communal support and assistance counteracts the isolation that the mourners might otherwise experience.

Admittedly, the exact historical origins of the rules, such as restrictions on shoes or the practice of covering mirrors, are not certain. My guess is that the majority of Jewish persons who observe these ritual practices do so because this is what Jews do when someone dies; the consolation of doing what one's ancestors and their ancestors did is itself important. However, one may be sceptical about the level of psychological satisfaction gained from sitting shiva by those for whom daily involvement with Jewish sacred law is nonexistent. Families with little knowledge or interest in Torah, in Jewish ways to marry, eat, pray, and study, will not be automatically comforted when entering into the Halakhah of mourning.

This seems obvious, but Christian pastoral counselors influenced by the death awareness movement frequently idealize and envy Jewish mourning. Their approach needs to be balanced with actual experiences of those who participate in these practices. As with the Japanese Buddhist rites, any long-term structuring of the bereavement period may make a difference, may help the mourners in an ongoing effort to recollect and reexperience the deceased, and gradually relinquish their old attachment to that person. Absence of such structure in American society in the twentieth century, rather than the specifics of what Jews or Japanese Buddhists do, is the real ground for envy. The same idealization and nostalgia can characterize descriptions of "old-time religion" in one's small town, where practices with no biblical basis nevertheless worked to structure mourning. ("You knew someone had died when you saw the minister's wife bring the Jello salad," one person put it wistfully.)

Yet, is a standardized pattern for mourning really what contemporary persons want or need? The death awareness movement has impacted on Christian funeral rites, has offered new psychological legitimations for Jewish practices, but is this enough? In the long run, the model of death as loss insists that each individual has experienced the loss uniquely; even when only one person has died, others' losses will be multiple. How can this awareness of the particularity of any one person's loss be encompassed by any standardized rite or practice?

V.

A pervasive contribution of the death awareness movement's focus on loss is to encourage the bereaved to create for themselves expressive rituals that memorialize the beloved dead, recollect, and reexperience relations to the lost person, and help them let go without forgetting. These rituals are never intended to appear in some future edition of *The Book of Common Prayer,* precisely because they are never "common," never communal-collective over time and place. Each family, each individual, ritualizes the loss uniquely. Some of these are suggested by counselors, some are spontaneous ideas of the bereaved, but all are intended to be expressions of personal feelings that accompany loss. They may involve gifts from the living to the dying, to show the specific way each survivor will miss the person who is leaving. A sense of completion, of memorializing, and of group cohesion mark the whole process. The creativity of different families and individuals must be matched by a relatively high degree of family unity. A bitterly divided group of mourners cannot accomplish the communication necessary to make this work. Although such rituals would normally be small-scale and private, this need not be the case. When Elton John rewrote the words of his song "Candle in the Wind" especially to perform at Princess Diana's funeral, millions of people grasped intuitively why such an expressive ritual, something done for this occasion, to remember this person only, is important.

Therapists and counselors can propose other kinds of expressive rituals where there has been silence, blocked grief, or anger. These are reminiscent of the Gestalt psychotherapy sessions of the 1960s, where an empty chair serves to locate the deceased as the presence still among the living, still part of their psychological world. The empty chair as the dead person is the invisible dialogue partner for the living, who one by one convey to him whatever unfinished business they need to transact. This level of expressive ritual uncovers and addresses negative emotions, unresolved conflicts, hidden guilt, and rage; it presupposes these forces already disrupt the lives of the mourners. (Alas, some of the most disrupted are very unlikely to accept invitations to participate in such therapeutic rites.) Nevertheless, since all relationships contain some negative aspects, a more private version of this "empty chair" group session is a ubiquitous technique in therapy and counseling with the bereaved. For the widow to write a letter to her dead husband, for instance, is a common suggestion. Perhaps initially the emotional tone will be angry or despairing, but once these feelings are given voice, other emotions can emerge: love, gratitude for what the relationship brought the survivor, increased trust in the latter's own resources to begin a new life.

The sole purpose of such therapeutic rituals is assistance to the bereaved. An interesting confrontation over these therapies resulted when an African pastor challenged their validity and orthodoxy. "How can you encourage Christians to communicate with the dead?" he wanted to know. In his society, he explained, to convert to Christianity meant to forsake sorcery, which includes all transactions with dead spirits. The baptized swore never to communicate with their dead ancestors for purposes of sorcery. "How can you therapists encourage something so dangerously close to forbidden practices?" he asked a startled meeting of Christian counselors. They replied that they do not believe that dead spirits are *really* being invoked, nor do they confuse the empty chair of the therapy session with anything from a seance. They assume that the separation of the dead from the living is a fact. What they attempt to accomplish is to deal with the internalized images of the dead held in the psyches of the mourners. These are psychically real but not literally the same as the dead person's soul or spirit. Nothing that the family members can say ("I hated you when you were alive, you were a terrible father, and I hate you now that you are dead!") can truly affect the dead person one way or another.

The therapeutically oriented participants and audience took this all for granted, until someone from outside North American culture questioned it. Once he spoke, it illuminated both the flexibility and the limit of the worldview shared by the death awareness movement and many contemporary American Christians. The dead are and remain dead, separated from real contact with the living. The dangers faced by the bereaved may occupy over six hundred pages in Rando's textbook, but do not include what the African pastor feared.

As expressive rituals focus on the needs of mourners to memorialize the dead, they connect with those most official monuments that have existed for many centuries: war memorials, gravestones, plaques, and tombs. But their expressive individualized dimension makes them different, less formal and more authentically linked to the particularities of individual mourners. The best example of the official style of memorial may be the Vietnam Memorial, but the best as well as the largest expressive and individualized memorial is the NAMES Project, commonly referred to as the AIDS Memorial Quilt. The former is stark, plain, with each name absolutely identical in lettering and size. The AIDS Quilt panels are also standardized in size, but the content is whatever each individual or group designs. Indeed, there may have been several panels for one deceased person, contributed by different individuals. A classical, traditional quilt is not, of course, simply a collection of separate

pieces endlessly added to one another, but a unified design of diverse patches. It has an organic unity that the AIDS Quilt lacks. On
the other hand, as the latter grew it became impossible to display
all at once; the quilt was divided and the sections of it sent on their
different ways for display in a wide range of places. The aim was
to involve as many persons as possible, to display the panels in as
many venues as possible, to keep the process of recollection ongoing, so long as the disease remained deadly.

At this point, the investigation of "death as loss" seems to have
come full circle, back to the struggle of American society to encounter loss, to come to terms with it, to mourn it. The two very
different memorials are expressions of this encounter, as, I have
argued, is the death awareness movement itself. Its success has
been to explore the reality of mourning, of the death of the other
as it is experienced by those who remain alive. Its theoretical
model is powerful in regard to this situation, but shakier and less
adequate when applied to the impending death of the self. Moreover, its impact has not been primarily in the space of hospital
practice, the ICU, and the hospice program, but in creating at least
some public awareness of the need to mourn, and some public
places and occasions to do so. Christian funeral liturgies have accepted and to some extent included this concern, but cannot simply substitute it for their own traditional images. Insofar as the rites
observed by Christians in this culture share in the dominant patterns of our culture, they have responded to the concerns of the
death awareness movement, without embracing the kind of link to
the dead that worried the African pastor.

Yet other, more traditional messages about death retain their
place, or ought to. "All we go down to the dust" is not invalidated
or replaced by concern for the comfort of those who mourn. The
newer psychologies of dying and death have not really replaced
this with a more adequate grasp of the situation of individual dying. The models of bereavement imposed as parallels onto that situation have not worked very well. Although death is indeed loss,
it remains more than this, and a spirituality of death and dying
ought to remain open to alternatives, even if these are not directly

derived from psychological models and practice. This does not require that *all* alternatives be maintained, or that some possibilities should not be discarded. But unless the loss motif is seen as one, rather than the totality of death's meanings, the range of images remains unexplored. The contribution of the death awareness movement has been substantial, but that is not the end of the story.

MEDITATION 4: MOURNERS AT THE CROSS
John 19:25–27

The three Synoptic Gospels omit all of Jesus' friends and followers from the crucifixion. The absence of Peter, John, and the others is blatant. Biblical scholars assume that such an important absence could never have been invented by the later community; indeed, these same persons would have had every reason to conceal or distort how completely they had deserted their dying Lord. It is testimony to the authenticity of these traditions that the future church leaders never made false claims about their own faithfulness at the time of Jesus' crucifixion.

The presence of mourners in John's Gospel becomes, then, an anomaly. Jesus' mother, her sister, and Mary Magdalene, along with the beloved disciple, remain as witnesses to his death. Here and here alone are real mourners, who stand and watch. If we allow this account validity in a wish to include mourners and bereavement into our comprehension of the passion, we face other dilemmas. Mourning, as we have seen, requires relationships. The only actual dialogue between Jesus and those who mourned him is directly about such relationships. Dying, he offers his beloved disciple to his mother as his replacement. "Dear woman, here is your son;" and then, to the disciple, "Here is your mother." The beloved disciple is there primarily as faithful witness to the death, but traditionally the role of principle mourner has been reserved for his mother. It is Mary whose sorrowful watch over her grown son's death has been elaborated in devotional and artistic expressions, regardless of how little attention mourning receives theologically. From the poem "Stabat Mater," incorporated into some versions of the Stations of the Cross, to Michelangelo's *Pieta,* this image of the Sorrowful Mother fills the space given to mourning in the passion.

Not only is this space gender-specific, it is also not Protestant space. Devotional identification with Mary is possible for those for whom she is Blessed Mother, Intercessor, Queen of Heaven. Those Protestant Christians now intrigued by Mary have been excited by these imageries of feminine power and authority. But the woman who grieves her dying son is and remains dependent upon him. She needs a son to survive, and the replacement she is given in the Gospel scene makes this clear. The Sorrowful Mother is not a particularly feminist Mary; she remains silent and passive as she watches her son die.

The other mourners include a woman whose role is even more controversial. Mary Magdalene is not only present at Jesus' death in John's account, but she becomes one of the first witnesses to the resurrection in all four Gospels. In the scene beginning with John 20:10, she is bereaved and weeping. She is the only nonmaternal named female figure linked to Jesus, and the limit set on her role as mourner is a limit set on how traditional sources could imagine their relationship. Was she in love with him? Yes. But never can the tradition pair the two of them in a relation that would allow Jesus a private, romantic, and erotic tie. To open up the topic of bereavement is to approach the human attachments of Jesus himself in a manner Christians have been squeamish about. The Jesus of the Gospels has friends, enjoys personal attachments, is able to relax in their homes—and so will naturally be missed and mourned by them. But this has not been the dominant way Christians who acknowledge him as Lord and Savior have wished to remember him. Even when much more attention is given to the human Jesus as a person in every way like us, many Christians remain reluctant to accept the consequences of this. The death awareness movement may have helped create space for loss and mourning, but Marian piety and Jesus' sexuality are two topics so controversial that as yet contemporary Protestants have not yet ventured to link the reality of loss with these details of the passion.

The other reason bereavement and loss have received so little due is that after Good Friday comes Easter. Proclaim Easter, the resurrection, the day of joy and triumph over death, and we won't need to spend time mourning. This line of thought leads directly to the liturgical revisions that were so pastorally inappropriate for funerals. It erases mourning from the available texts, and from the range of permissable situations and experiences. The Gospels do indeed proclaim the resurrection, but we should beware of this line of argument. There is space for mourners at the foot of the cross — controversial and biased toward women, but space nevertheless.

5

What's Missing?
The Disappearance
of Death as Punishment

I.

In this book, I examine the outlines and emphases of the death awareness movement, relating its new words for dying, death, and loss to those available to Christians now and in the past. The focus is on what the new resurgence of interest in dying and death has contributed that was not present before the 1960s. Three possible outcomes can occur when anything new is said: it may be that what is old remains, side by side with the new; or that what is new aims directly to replace what is old, and for a while a conflict rages between partisans of the old and the new; or that something once present is now gone, having gone quietly enough so that no one notices its absence. In this chapter, I look at imagery and ideas that do not appear in the death awareness movement, and that also seem to have dropped out of the Christian theological picture prior to that movement's beginning.

Death as punishment, death as judgment by God for sin, death as sin's "wages." These ideas have a dismal weight, so that even to write of them is dreary. Like the topic of divine wrath, to which they are related, they fill some persons with anger. An image of Hell, judgment, guilt, wrath, and judicial penalty looms up before us. Who needs this, when death is already frightening enough and dying difficult enough in the high-tech hospital setting? When mourning is already a lifelong, complex coming to terms with loss? Ivan Ilych struggling in his misery and isolation is not being punished from outside himself by God; he is in agony from within, confronting and becoming a self in the face of death. When he acknowledges that his life has not been a good one, it is not because he has experienced God as judge condemning him.

In the contemporary death awareness movement, ideas of punishment and judgment have utterly vanished. Even the pastoral care literature influenced by the movement reflects this absence. Since death is natural, what would be "unnatural" is a death-free existence, an endless life, a story in time without closure. Within nature's realm, there is a time to be born and a time to die. Within its horizon, it makes no sense at all to single out human deaths and claim for these a special status as "sin's wages," as punishment for disobedience. No matter how subtly and nonliterally such ideas are presented, they do not fit, they will never combine with a vision of death as natural event.

On the other hand, if we as Christians are literalists, the story of the Fall guides our thinking about such matters. Adam and Eve were created free, finite, and undying. They lived in harmony, as vegetarians but with peaceful dominion over all other creatures. Without birth, they were also without death. Then they "fell," they broke trust with God and with each other. Their immediate response was guilt and shame. But death came upon them, along with hard work and painful childbirth, as punishment from outside, ordained by God. Their life in the world of time and death is a life of exile, for they were banished from their original home and left to grow old and die outside its gates. How could life have developed within Eden? Could existence outside mortality have been both creative and stable, without boredom or arrogance? What would a death-free human being be like? Such a person—part of God's Plan A, which came unglued at the Fall—is never part of our human existence, even postsalvation.

Interestingly, it is also never part of the Hebrew Bible's vision, for except in that one chapter of Genesis, there is no interest in viewing death in itself as punishment. The mortality of human beings is elsewhere entirely taken for granted. Like the grass in the field, humans live but for a short while, while the Lord endures forever.

> You sweep men away in the sleep of death;
> they are like the new grass of the morning—
> though in the morning it springs up new,
> by evening it is dry and withered.
>
> (Psalm 90:5)

Even when the prophets envision a redeemed humanity, freed of injustice and at peace, they include a full life but also a timely death.

> Never again will there be in it
> an infant who lives but a few days,
> or an old man who does not live out his years.
>
> (Isa. 65:20)

Not deathlessness, but freedom from premature or violent death is the most appropriate hope.

Nevertheless, in case anyone wishes to idealize this vision as both biblical and natural, there is a lot of "death as punishment" throughout these same scriptures. "Bad deaths," to use Lloyd Bailey's phrase,[1] include instances of those who die violently, struck down directly as a result of their disobedience. Another "bad death" is that of the childless man, who will lack descendants to remember him and honor his name. Although death in general is not considered a punishment, there is surely space for particular deaths to receive this meaning. The death of Joab, David's hated violent commander, is one example; when his royal protector dies, he flees to an altar, pursued by Solomon's men. Solomon orders Joab struck down. "The Lord will repay him for the blood he shed. . . . May the guilt of their blood rest on the head of Joab and his descendants forever" (1 Kings 2:32–33). This kind of death is clearly exceptional, but it separates the Hebrew view of death from contemporary ideas of natural death.

How do Christians move beyond these options? Are Christians irrevocably committed to some inclusion of punishment or

judgment in regard to death? If so, why has this not been an issue of direct conflict with the death awareness movement? The
reaction against such imagery began long before the death
awareness movement as a shift in Christian theology in the nineteenth century. Miller-McLemore states:

> When the ideas of authority, duty, punishment and morality be-
> came increasingly unpopular . . . theologians ceased struggling
> with the relations between these ideas and death. The disap-
> pearance of the judgmental view of death has had its obvious
> liberating consequences. . . .

However, she adds that this leaves "a vacuum that psychology and
medicine fill with new moralisms,"[2] so that "people in general no
longer have language to talk about the moral dimension" of death.[3]
Why is some connection of death with sin and judgment—while
neither popular nor desirable in itself—in some way necessary for
Christians to retain?

Theologians struggling to go beyond "death is natural" believe
that it is important to retain some sense of death's weight, its negativity, its more-than-natural link to fundamental human anxiety
over moral and existential limits. Even if the traditional language
of judgment and punishment is no longer appropriate, "we cannot
abandon the concept of sin, especially in relation to death."[4] But
why not? Should death be treated with awe? Does it require a kind
of sacred space at the brink of life's ending? If so, why does it need
the connection to sin? Death can have a sacred and moral dimension even as natural event without carrying with it any of the negative sense of sin's wages. To understand better what is at stake in
the disappearance of punishment and judgment imagery, we need
to briefly review its role in the New Testament, in images that became the starting places for intense theological elaborations.

II.

The imagery of death as punishment for sin plays an entirely
different role in the New Testament than in the Old. Not only does

Paul use "Adam" and his sin as the starting place for rhetorical contrasts between pre- and post-Christ existence, but the specific links between death, sin, and punishment are stated directly:

> Just as sin entered the world through one man, and death through sin, and in this way death came to all men, because all sinned. . . . But the gift is not like the trespass. For if the many died by the trespass of the one man, how much more did God's grace and the gift that came by the grace of the one man, Jesus Christ, overflow to the many! . . . The judgment followed one sin and brought condemnation, but the gift followed many trespasses and brought justification. (Rom. 5:12, 15–16)

Justification is a legal term; God as judge declares the accused party righteous. Although as sinners we were condemned to death, now that Christ has come, God's verdict of justification has set us in a new situation, of life and not death. The death that is referred to here is both mortality, the situation of all humans, and a kind of capital punishment, instituted by God as judge. This strand of New Testament imagery became historically important especially in the West. I read such passages as this by surrounding them with the "paratext" of Luther and Reformation debates about justification by faith. Neither Paul nor Luther were focused explicitly and exclusively on death, but the death-sin connection plays a vital role for both in their presentation of the gospel.

This is actually only one strand of New Testament imagery for salvation through Christ. Another is Christ's death as a sacrifice. As Lamb of God, he is slain for the sins of the world. His death, construed this way, focuses on religious categories such as expiation and propitiation, for sacrifices of various kinds were the sacred acts that restored right relations between God and humans. To offer sacrifices was to reestablish fellowship, to undo trespasses and pollutions, and make clean what had been defiled. The offering of blood releases power to set the person who offers it on the road of life, not death. Death as sacrifice is complex; it is not as simple as "God is angry, someone's got to pay." It involves categories of trespass, violation, and fault. Jesus' death as sacrifice takes up these images. His death releases power, and restores the fundamental relationship with God that had been broken. Sacrifice is not by itself a legal category, but it is shaped by the legal language of transgression and guilt.

Both these sets of images in the early church and the New Testament derive, I am certain, from the specific circumstances of Jesus' own death. The death of Jesus was a capital punishment, a legal execution. It was also bloody and violent. Its timing to coincide with Passover contributed to these connections too. Jesus' extraordinarily unnatural death, at the hands of legally constituted authorities, meant that for Christians the meanings of this death would be inextricably tied up to questions about justice and judgment, guilt and innocence. Atonement, justification, redemption, salvation: a marvelous complex patchwork of images and concepts arose around this death and its meanings. The starting point for Christian reflection on death begins from a judicial punishment, suffered by a crucified Messiah.

But why should Paul and other Christians after him have been so insistent that judicial categories worked for all deaths? Why should we all be guilty before God and condemned to death? Why interpret the human situation this way? Jesus' own ministry had centered on the call to repentance and preparation for the kingdom of God; this assumes a need for repentance, a state of sin from which God can release us. But Jesus himself does not seem to be preoccupied with this condition. "If you then who are evil know how to give good gifts to your children, then how much more will God . . . " (Luke 11:13). The lost sheep, the lost coin: parables emphasize the urgent love of God for the sinner, but without elaboration. Yes, there will be a future judgment in which sheep and goats, wheat and weeds, will be separated and the latter destroyed. But all of these examples could have been taken as evidence that sinfulness is unequally parcelled out; there are sheep who do not stray, and wheat grows abundantly in the field. Every example where God seeks the sinner's healing could be balanced by examples of those who need no physician.

But something comes between these examples and the message we have heard from Paul. A horrendous death and a glorious yet

mysterious resurrection slant all interpretations of these parables
away from such readings. We are all the lost sheep, we are all in
dire need of redemption from a world where the Lamb of God was
slain. This is a world whose rulers judged and condemned the one
who will one day judge the world. The law's righteousness, like the
world's wealth and success, became for Paul rubbish in the light of
knowing Christ. From within this light, the deathliness of death and
the sinfulness of sin looked more universally destructive and evil.
From within this light, the gift overcomes the trespass, and the trespass itself is seen fully for the first time. This relationship helps explain why Paul's statements about "Adam" are always set in the
midst of a contrast between the "man from earth" and the "man
from heaven" (1 Cor. 15:47), not between Adam in Paradise and
Adam after the fall. The appearance of Christ shifts the whole landscape, and forces revisioning of all that came before.

But if this is so, as a statement about the format of Christian theology, it also implies that one cannot simply omit punishment language in regard to death, and go on with things as before. The
language of judicial condemnation and of sacrifice places us in the
midst of central beliefs and hopes of Christian faith. What happens
when judgment and punishment imagery disappear from Christian
language about death is part of a larger picture in Western Christianity, which includes revisions of the message in regard to other
topics. Although the Reformation had deepened the meaning of
some of this judicial language in all the debates about justification
and imputed righteousness, by the nineteenth century this imagery
no longer went unquestioned.

Could Christian thought be reframed to omit or translate terms
such as these into other images? The reason given by theologian
Albert Ritschl to discard all legal language in regard to salvation
has no explicit link with death. Writing in 1870, Ritschl states categorically that "The designation of God as our Father shows ex-
pressly that the real analogy for the Kingdom of God should be
sought, not in the national State, but in the family."[5] The ruler of
a state may occasionally pardon a criminal, although the normal
workings of justice do not require it. In contrast, the loving father

always loves his children, always works for their best, and always forgives them. This is pre-Freud; today one might be less sanguine about the purity and innocence of family love, but nevertheless still find intimate bonds the only appropriate metaphors for God's saving presence, while "the national State" is excluded as a source of metaphors.

I select this example deliberately because Ritschl's distrust of the national and political dimension of the kingdom of God is itself part of the story. Legal imagery of condemnation, the normal power of the judicial system, requires a public dimension to what God accomplishes. Family, Ritschl's substitute, is private, a set of intimate personal links of love. To let go of the former images is to leave the gospel without connection to the larger institutional patterns of society at a time when these structures became vastly more powerful and influential than before. If Christians no longer wanted to speak of a "kingdom," the national states of Europe were eager to organize and evoke idolatrous loyalties. Inability to say anything about politics and national life may have resulted from this shrinkage of metaphors. It privatizes and falsely spiritualizes the family, while ignoring the claims of justice and public power within the political world.

Ritschl was aware that he chose between images, both of which are powerful and have some claim to validity. In discussing death, however, most often those who have chosen between "death as natural" and "death as punishment for sin" have not been so self-aware. In chapter 2, I made clear that "death as natural" is itself an image with a moral dimension of its own, with limits and possibilities like all other images. As an image, it helps us see some things well, while it closes other windows and pathways to human experiences. Just as Ritschl's decision to discard the national state implied in kingdom language closed off political realities, so when Christians began to avoid judgment and punishment language for death, it became hard to see and say the realities that persist as "the moral life."

The death awareness movement did not initiate rejection of judgment and punishment as categories for grasping death. Those nineteenth-century thinkers who did could not have anticipated how the modern hospital would become a problematic new arena for awareness of death's reality and presence. However, the death awareness movement's insistence on death as natural event and death as loss has continued and intensified this process, so that in the next stage of this rejection, "the moral life" in some of its specifics becomes even more difficult to discuss.

III.

In this section, I take up the story of the absence of punishment language by looking at a few situations where this has been either disputed, or where the death awareness movement's limitations have led to a vacuum filled in by other forces. It is not my aim to restore all the traditional language of death as punishment for sin, but by citing the problems of that language's absence, one may begin to grasp what the traditional judicial categories and images accomplished. Recall how universal and sweeping the Pauline version of those ideas is. *All* death comes from Adam, *every* human shares Adam's trespass, and so its consequences. If *any* death is a punishment, then this is primarily because *every* death is. This, as we have seen, is already a contrast with the Hebrew Bible's stories in which the death of David is a good death while that of Joab is truly punishment. When Christian theology discards judicial language in its general categories, it also assumes that treatment of individual deaths shifts automatically. The difference between good and bad deaths was already erased, so to speak, by Jesus' utterly "bad" but totally salvific death. No theologian who, like Ritschl, avoided legal and penalty language ever imagined that some deaths were still to be treated as especially punitive, as verdicts from God.

Morally problematic deaths may never have been so completely banished from Christian exhortation and practical evangelism as this stating of the problem assumes. The awful deaths of sinners, the premature deaths of the young and ungodly, were the stock of public preaching and pastoral counseling down through the ages.

In other words, that *all* death was punishment for sin did not prevent the sudden violent death of a notoriously wicked person from being gleefully proclaimed as proof of God's justice. Stories in the Acts of the Apostles of just this sort show that focus on particular bad deaths did not by any means disappear with the coming of the gospel. It continued, with elaborations of what a truly bad death might entail. For example, a collection of deathbed scenes made by a pastor who had worked among victims of a nineteenth-century epidemic separates "good deaths" and the "deaths of sinners." He adds a special section on "The Deaths of Worldly Churchmen," for whom remorse and shame were especially intense.[6] Nevertheless, the more universal language of theological doctrines relativize these divisions. Everyone dies, all share in Adam's sin and in the need for salvation.

Today, however, morally problematic deaths do not receive this level of attention. The death awareness movement has its own ideal of an acceptable death, and its own version of a bad death (one that is marked by fear, denial, isolation, and medical tyranny), but it lacks the conceptual resources to identify and address many other morally problematic situations. Deaths by suicide, murder, warfare, and preventable accidents are all losses, and our mourning for them will be complicated more often than for ordinary "natural" deaths. Unfortunately, from within the psychological spirituality of the death awareness literature, that is almost all that can be said. Some of these deaths are so unacceptable by any ordinary standard that it seems a travesty to call on "acceptance" as a general goal. When faced with really horrifying deaths, such as the murders of children, is the more morally adequate response acceptance or continued rage? And what of the murderers' reactions? To raise these kinds of questions shows how the death awareness movement's limited vision of good death versus bad death is restricted to issues of how personal control and family relationships are maintained as over against the helplessness and isolation of the hospital milieu. Other situations reveal a lack of language to address them adequately at all. Although it was never the intention of the death awareness movement to trivialize any death situation, the vocabulary of natural event, loss, acceptance, and of the emotional process of coming to terms with loss, cannot by itself begin to sort through when deaths are justified and when they are unjustified.

But if this is true for the situation of murder, then it extends to a range of situations addressed by the death awareness movement outside the framework of judicial or punishment categories. Take, for instance, some of the situations of disenfranchised grief. Disenfranchised grief is already a moral concept, premised as it is on the ideal of grief as legitimate and on the fundamental human right to feel and express loss. All grief should be enfranchised, even that which occurs in the midst of morally problematic situations such as extramarital affairs or abortion. Within this model, death is a loss no matter what the other circumstances and no matter what other perspectives could be invoked to grasp a particular death and bereavement. The counselor's job is to honor the grief, to enfranchise it, if not in public at least in the private space of therapy. For the counselor, this role does not lead to any direct conflict stemming from the morally problematic situation itself. For the funeral director, however, the ethics of the situation are not so clearcut. A mistress present at the viewing will add to the grief of the wife; negotiating for who can come when is a familiar part of the director's job.[7] Here, by the way, we have exactly that situation which the "invisible harmony" ethic that permeates self-actualization models of psychology cannot cover. Each griever's grief may need to be expressed and respected, but to honor one dishonors and further saddens the other. From within the perspective of disenfranchised grief, where the only category available is death as loss, the full disruption of claims in conflict cannot be seen or resolved.

There are other deaths where categories of judicial penalty seem to belong but for which the death awareness movement does not in itself provide language to guide those involved. The enormous rise in medical malpractice suits is usually attributed to the demise of paternalism in medicine, an oversupply of lawyers, and the fascination of Americans with personal rights. Malpractice is a legal category, but it must involve the judgment that someone is to blame, that a bad outcome is not just fate but culpability. Someone died, someone was misdiagnosed, someone's surgery was done badly—and this was not due to fate or the inherent limits of knowledge, but to ignorance among those who should have known, or carelessness by those who claim expertise. There are cases where these judgments may be easy to make. There are many where they are not. Moreover, the real issue may also be whether those who suffer the bad outcome should decide to pursue the route of malpractice litigation just because someone with legal training says that the case is "actionable." Is a malpractice suit worth the human cost, even if there is a potential of financial recompense? To enter this territory, one needs to see the limits of medicine, and also the limits of the legal system. One needs to address issues of blame and responsibility, and acknowledge that while a particular death may be unacceptable to us personally, it need not necessarily be anyone's fault. If when someone dies I am sure that someone else must have made a mistake and therefore must be made to pay, is my thinking due to a continued vision of death as unacceptable or impossible—an unnatural outcome for which we have no social and spiritual space? The death awareness movement has tried to move beyond this stance. But does the proliferation of medical malpractice suits show how "death as unnatural" still holds sway? Judicial language banished from theology and outside the death awareness movement may have returned, enacted literally through the courts.

IV.

There is another, more controversial, and I might even say more sinister set of deaths within which punishment and judgment language plays a role, however adamantly the death awareness movement resists such usage. These are the deaths that in some way were caused or hastened by human behavior, where the relationship between disease and moral life seems to be present, however complex and ambiguous it may be. The most infamous example is the claim that AIDS is God's punishment against homosexuals, which is also the only instance I know of where the full weight of divine authority is invoked to make this connection between a deadly disease as punishment for sinful behavior. But the AIDS example is not truly unique in other ways. The judgment that smokers have only themselves to blame for dying of lung cancer is not linked to God, but the idea that behavior, blame, and death all belong together is parallel to the AIDS example. When such arguments are used, those who voice them are usually careful to make exceptions for the persons who caught the disease "innocently." Hemophiliacs sickened by tainted blood transfusions, infants infected in utero, and those exposed to secondhand smoke are all victims in a sense that others were not, according to this logic. Moreover, in an additional refinement of the original idea, some factor of increasing medical information available will be added to the argument; a distinction may be offered between those who behaved badly while in ignorance about the dangers, and those who knew—about AIDS or about the risks of smoking—but who went ahead and acted without regard to that knowledge.

These two examples are not isolated from a wider range of others. In all cases where lifestyle is somehow linked to disease through diet, exercise, sexual behavior, alcohol consumption, and drug use, the efforts for prevention will have to focus directly on these matters. Sexual examples are more highly charged than others, but matters of cholesterol and fat intake require exactly the same exhortations regarding free personal choices. It may be my right as an American citizen to eat french fries three times a day, but when I develop heart disease or high blood pressure, I will have participated in bringing on these illnesses. In addition, insofar as I risk my own health I also create an unnecessary burden for others: my family and the taxpayers who must foot part of the bill for my medical care. By taking responsibility for my own health and wellness I gain increased sense of control over my life, but I also must stand publicly accountable for behavior that, from another point of view, is strictly my own private business. A language of personal rights exists to counteract almost any attempt to deal with these issues as public problems.

Admittedly, taking responsibility for one's own health and wellness is just one piece of a complex issue. In many of the above cases, there are parties for whom the dangerous behavior was or remains profitable business. Owners of gay baths early in the AIDS epidemic, and tobacco companies all along, have a direct stake in keeping the behaviors popular, in keeping their customers confused and ignorant about the links between human action and disease. Government regulatory agencies, in turn, may have been in denial, or unwilling to tackle controversial powerful lobbies. A simple and by now well-known example is the official recommendation for a healthy diet. When I was growing up, the school's chart of equal-sized rectangular boxes for the "four basic food groups" made it seem as if equal amounts of meat and vegetables were to be eaten for a balanced diet. How was I to know that this was a misrepresentation, due not to sheer ignorance but to heavy lobbying by the beef industry? A more accurate chart has since appeared as a pyramid, with vegetables near the base and meat near the peak. So a strictly individualistic focus on personal responsibility is not entirely adequate, although most exhortations for prevention must start here.

Add to this the reality that few of these cause-and-prevention relationships are automatic and inevitable. No matter how many times some gay men engaged in promiscuous unprotected sex in the 1970s and early 1980s, they did not become infected with HIV. No matter how heavily they smoke, some persons will live to a very advanced age and die of something unrelated to tobacco. There is no one-to-one relationship between behavior and these partially preventable illnesses, and if our definitions of justice require that it work in every case identically, without exceptions, then these situations will never appear to warrant any of the language of judgment and punishment. Nevertheless, for many persons this is not exactly required for the punishment motif to be applicable. Certain behaviors have an established track record of medical risks; they carry destruction for those who engage in them enough of the time to warrant such judgment. The rhetoric of prevention depends on this.

But after the fact, once someone is already sick with a terminal or life-threatening illness, what happens to the issue of blame and behavior? Once sick, should someone be reminded that she brought this on herself? Should she feel guilt because she is truly guilty? Death awareness workers and writers note how often the language of blame is misapplied, such as when patients insist that they caught cancer from someone else and then blame that person, while ignoring medical evidence that this is impossible. Irrational blaming makes death awareness advocates even more opposed to ruminations of moral guilt among the dying. There is no encouragement to dwell on illness as punishment within this literature.

One option has been to transfer the language of personal responsibility for one's own behavior onto the task of getting well, or at least on surviving as long as possible. On this latter point, the death awareness movement has been divided and partially caught in a trap of its own making. Anxious to increase the patient's sense of control, especially in the midst of the hospital setting, it is easy to overemphasize the extent to which individuals have it in their power to take control over their illnesses, to become and remain activists in pursuit of healing. This activist stance can combine with the military model of fighting death and refusing to accept its inevitability that death awareness advocates find deeply problematic. When is taking responsibility a heroic ideal, and when is it finally one more expression of denial?

This is why the mainstream death awareness movement has been so ambivalent about calls to "heal yourself," to "take control" over your body, your illness, your healthy recovery. The now-classic *Anatomy of an Illness* by Norman Cousins recounts the tale of how the author, given a hopeless medical prognosis, succeeded in curing himself through laughter, through positive attitude, through an active involvement in his own treatment.[8] This story became an inspiration for a generation of patients; a positive, activist stance would triumph, or at least improve one's chances, no matter what the diagnosis. From this perspective, personal behavior might not have been a factor to note in how one acquired the illness, but a call for taking control and responsibility once sick was always appropriate in how one responded to illness.

This may sound very far away from "AIDS is God's punishment for homosexuality." Note that it is not entirely free from its own moral stance. A positive attitude is an obligation, and to maintain one consistently requires moral effort, which becomes one's duty. To fail in this, to let oneself sink back into illness and despair, is to fail morally just as surely as to engage in behavior that may have brought on or contributed to the illness. Indeed, as Cousins' model became grossly oversimplified, this dimension of the message became far more prominent and problematic. Those who get well have refused to be victims and have shown responsibility and activism, while those who succumb are weak, irresponsible, or perhaps just do not want to get well.

The death awareness movement, although it stresses the patient's own experience, never condones these implications. It avoids the metaphysics in which the world follows the pathway of immanent justice, in which virtually nothing is just bad luck and nothing can be undeserved. Indeed, long before this point, hospice workers and counselors of the dying were dismayed by the level of denial popular writers promoted, and how the promise of "self-healing" blocked any realistic reckoning with the inevitable progress of the disease. Yet the fluctuating popularity of such claims appears side by side with the death awareness movement's more mainstream, cautious, and somber perspective. Just as theology did not want to reconnect with the past sets of images focused on death as punishment for sin, the death awareness movement did not want to move beyond natural event and loss. But other voices arose that claimed to link death to justice, to punishment, to the moral life in some fashion: the voices of lawyers focusing on blame and reparation, of health educators intent to link behavior and disease, of those who claim that illness itself is always a moral flaw. These voices show how impossible it is to maintain a strict separation between death and the moral life. The absence of such language from some sources cannot prevent or control its reappearance elsewhere. If so, then the story should not be the absence of death as punishment for sin from Christian theology or from the death awareness movement, but its vigorous and contemporary resurgence outside these frameworks, and in forms that appear to be far more morally problematic than those now silenced.

I have intentionally left out a positive case for the idea of death as punishment for sin and themes of judgment, based on pastoral or spiritual grounds. It is one thing to note that there are inappropriate contemporary rediscoveries of judgment and punishment imagery. It is a negative argument to attribute these to the absence of strong theological messages on these themes. After all, at the level of pastoral practice and spiritual guidance, Ivan Ilych hardly needed more than what his despairing self-condemnation could offer. This replaces traditional judgment by God, but no one should doubt that the result can be just as horrifying. What Tolstoy's story shares with Bunyan's sensitive account of the righteous Christian's difficult river crossing is also worth stating: the final outcome of the struggle remains entirely secret in both cases. No obvious immanent justice is visible to the world at large. Those who wish to revitalize and validate traditional images of death as punishment for sin should, I believe, keep this reminder of God's hidden, awesome presence and power before them.

MEDITATION 5: JUSTLY AND UNJUSTLY PUNISHED
Luke 23:39–43

Jesus dies a judicial and not a natural death. Sharing this death are two ordinary criminals. If there are mourners at the crucifixion only in John's account, these two executed alongside Jesus speak only in Luke's. To take the judicial imagery for death seriously is to connect our own deaths to theirs. This is clearly intended by the Gospel narrator. Without this imagery, the anger of the first criminal and the acceptance of the second would be meaningless.

Hanging side by side on their crosses, the two criminals and Jesus are all equally condemned, and will die side by side. The first finds in Jesus' presence a source of extra anger. "Aren't you the Christ? Save yourself and us!" he cries out. It is evil enough to die of capital punishment in a public execution. To do so together with one who just might have an inside deal for escape, but who refuses to try it, is unbearable. The unfairness and injustice of Jesus' death is not the issue for this man. He, like Kübler-Ross's hospital patients, finds the idea of sacrificial death completely meaningless. If someone can live, live! Don't die needlessly.

So, too, Albert Camus in *The Plague* finds such glorification of injustice impossible to accept. It is always wrong to give up the struggle; it is always wrong to glorify and mystify evil by consenting and collaborating with it.[9] If you can save yourself and others, you must try. From this viewpoint, the first criminal speaks truly, and his bitterness is valid. There is no justice in death, and one who assents to its injustice is sharing in the evil of the executioners.

The second criminal reveals the opposite attitude. His death is as physically and mentally punishing and unnatural as those of the others on their crosses. Yet his reply to the first man stands as the purest, clearest statement of how judicial imagery for death has worked. "Don't you fear God," he said, "since you are under the same sentence? We are punished justly, for we are getting what our deeds deserve. But this man has done nothing wrong." These are words that all other human beings, from Adam onwards, could say of themselves. God, in fact, desires this. Our deaths are what our deeds deserve. It does not matter that we may die from a medical cause completely unrelated to particular legally designated crimes. The exact mode of our death is completely irrelevant, for we all die of sin, justly sentenced and punished. Only Jesus dies innocent, a true victim who deserves a better end. He shares in our death, but never in our guilt.

The death awareness movement can make nothing of either the first or the second man's words, nor of the entire issue behind these. Camus could understand the issue, and protest against the kind of moral topsy-turvy that masochistically finds the glorification of injustice a satisfying cosmic principle. The death awareness advocates and those pastoral care writers influenced by them cannot really wrestle with Camus's protest either. The three unnatural deaths on Golgotha cannot be paradigms for anything; they are not to be models for our dying. They should not begin to play the roles traditionally given them, of exemplifying the link between death, sin, and guilt. All humans expect to die, but we are not to construct meanings around this natural fact that turn it into a legal sentence, a just or injust punishment, or a grim consequence for what our deeds deserve.

The death awareness movement cannot accept the first criminal's bitter accusation. If death is above all a natural event, a biological and universal given, then it is ridiculous to expect to be saved from it. Nor can it truly be just or injust. The anger of the first criminal, like all other anger in dying, is an expression of his own need for control and attention. It is a response to his own fear. He projects it onto Jesus not because he genuinely accepts that Jesus is the Messiah, but because Jesus is the nearest available human target for his outburst of wrath. The only real question for the angry dying person is "Why me?"—a question to which no reasonable answer is really expected or wanted.

The second criminal's response is even more distant from the vision of the death awareness advocates. Perhaps coming to terms with his own guilt helps him resolve reactive depression and complete his dying by wrapping up unfinished business. This is not nothing; it is a positive step and removes an obstacle to his dying. But there is no connection between his reminder "Don't you fear God?" and the language of the death awareness movement. To fear God, to accept that one is being justly punished by both the civil authorities and by God, is outside the boundaries of what the contemporary death awareness movement can consider as valid or helpful for the dying.

And now, how does Jesus fit between the two criminals? He has earlier, in verse 34, forgiven his executioners or, rather, asked God to forgive them. He does more here than complete unfinished emotional business. He acknowledges that injustice has been done, but lays aside personal bitterness, and asks that those guilty of injustice will be spared the punishment for what *their deeds* deserve. But it is in his interaction with the second criminal that the true solution to the problem of death as punishment for sin is revealed.

When the repentant criminal turns to Jesus and begs him, "Remember me when you come into your kingdom," Jesus replies, "I tell you the truth, today you will be with me in Paradise." Dying together, they will share in eternal life together. The guilt that led to death will not remain a barrier to salvation. As Jesus comes into his kingdom, he comes to open its gate to all those who died guilty. His death lifts the punishment from all who call to him in faith. The second criminal is thus given the honor of being the first full human example of completed salvation, the first one who will join with Jesus in the kingdom of eternal life.

Is this difficult for us to grasp? It may be so because the death awareness movement has closed it off to us, shut down a level of imagery and meaning that the story makes central. Camus could understand this imagery, although he and many others in the modern period have found it unbearable, a travesty of true justice. How can we reopen this imagery, so that it becomes again a real insight into dying and death for us? A way to do this is to imagine an ending to the story in which the irrelevance of justice and punishment language is taken to its absolute extreme, in which such concerns are denied any role at the highest and most absolute level. In this scenario, the second criminal outlasts Jesus on the cross, but dies and arrives at the gate of Paradise. Inside, Jesus already sits in glory at the right hand of the Father, ruler of the kingdom promised to him. The dead criminal begs for entrance, based on the promise made at Golgotha. Yet Jesus somehow has now forgotten the last painful details of his life on earth, and pays no heed to him. The injustices of his death are ignored, blocked out, and with this, the memory of the promise to save the one who called out to him for help when near death. Justice and punishment no longer matter after all, but then the potential injustice of breaking such a promise is also irrelevant. In this version, abandonment of all imagery from judicial categories is consistent, but with this goes all language of debt and obligation as well. Such an ending would be a deeper injustice, a monstrous unworthy trick. It makes Jesus and his Father more worthy of condemnation than the second criminal, whatever the man's original offenses for which he received his death sentence. (Franz Kafka's parable "Before the Law" actually tells this kind of story, taking us deep into the pathology of punishment without redemption.[10])

When I add this possibility to the story as Luke has written it, I find that the meaning of faith as trust expands to include death as punishment, the whole range of judgment and penalty imagery. A vision of a God who forgets and simply rises up above all such concerns is also that of a God for whom betrayal of a promise is a possibility. In the story, I am given a choice as to whether to follow the way of the first criminal and die in bitter anger against God, or whether to turn to Jesus and trust that he can open the gate to his kingdom and receive me there. Luke offers these two paths to anticipate and experience my own death. What makes the latter pathway a real option is that Jesus is just and trustworthy, able to fulfill what he promises and interested in doing so. When I recognize this, I may not have restored the entire post-Augustinian framework for death as punishment for sin, but I have reopened a vision of divine justice that can be truthfully linked to death.

What's Missing?
The Absence of the Afterlife

I.

The landscape of faith drawn by John Bunyan and traversed by his pilgrims was bounded by two cities: the City of Destruction, from which they all fled, and the Celestial City, toward which they all walked. Bunyan was not being original; he adopted a traditional image of life as a pilgrimage within this world, while at the end lay a sacred goal. Another image to capture that relationship is supplied by Dante's cosmology; here we are on earth's surface, the "dark wood" of the initial cantos. Once the poet enters the three eternal realms, the dead from all eras and places mingle together, separated by their moral/spiritual status, but outside historical time as it exists on earth. These traditional visionary portraits make sense of life here on earth by including destinations beyond this world and after death. While neither of these pictures may be truly in tune with the deepest intentions of the New Testament, their influence has been pervasive. The dead have both a destiny and a destination beyond this life.

For many persons, this and only this defines what "religion" covers. Without concern for Heaven, my students often say, there would be no point or meaning to religion at all. Yet it is also clear that for these same young adults, Heaven plays no role in their day-to-day lives, has no Dantean reality as an eternal presence above their world of school, part-time jobs, and summers at the shore with their friends. Heaven is invoked upon the occasion of death, but it is a belief without moorings to practices in life. A religion without an afterlife would be unimaginable to them, just as would any version of Christianity that defined eternal life so that ultimacy and divine presence *now* replaced or partly replaced the image of a heavenly afterlife.

The Heaven they accept has much more in common with nineteenth-century sentimental piety than it does with Dante or the Bible. Heaven became the place where one met one's beloved dead. God, Jesus, and angels were there, of course, but they became less important than the anticipated reunions with one's own family members. Elizabeth Phelps's best-selling *The Gates Ajar* (1868) rebuilt Christian visions of Heaven through the principle of wishful analogy: anything good or pleasant on earth will be available in Heaven, not in spiritualized transfigured form, but exactly as enjoyed in this life.[1] Family relationships, aesthetic pleasures, restful recreation— Phelps's Heaven was cluttered with these. Because it lacked work, Phelps's Heaven looks uncannily like today's retirement communities, although the former's inhabitants include many young people. My students have in mind the same notion of a place where Grandma and Pop-Pop can now be together again. This is certainly the portrait that emerges from the memorial pages of the *South Philadelphia Review-Chronicle,* where letters to the dead assume that family ties and yearly celebrations continue in the afterlife. "Happy 30th Wedding Anniversary to Mom and Dad in Heaven" such letters read, signed by the kids, the grandkids, the great-grandkids. Jesus' statement that there is no marrying or giving in marriage in the kingdom of God (Matt. 22:30) apparently does not apply to the South Philadelphia section. Dead children still celebrate birthdays, receive Christmas presents, and even go trick-or-treating in this local variant of Heaven-by-analogy. Some things, however, are not transferrable. A dead adolescent does not get his driver's license in Heaven, perhaps because this would signify the growth into adult independence that the whole imagery tries to counteract. Dead pets are sometimes memorialized, but do not get located in "dog heaven," at least not in the newspaper. Moreover, the weight of these memorials is not, as in Phelps, the happy anticipation of reunions in Heaven. It is, true to contemporary sensibilities, the reality of the loss for those left behind. "We know that you are together again, but we miss you here on earth" is the typical message.

Why begin an examination of the afterlife's absence from the death awareness movement here? Because that absence is also a feature of contemporary Christianity, albeit in a peculiar way. Many twentieth-century systematic theologians revived and reinterpreted eschatology so that it no longer referred to the traditional last things of death, judgment, Heaven, and Hell. Eschatology became the ultimate transcendent dimension of all reality in the midst of *this* life. It became a way to talk about God's plan and final purpose for the creation, rather than focusing upon personal death. Debates over what constituted biblical eschatology took place in a theological arena dominated by conflicting visions of history, of secular universal utopias, of war and mass destruction in Europe, and the end of colonialism abroad. Attention to personal, individual death seemed small-scale, if not selfish.[2] The theologians wished to relocate and redefine eternal life so that an eternal, divine presence was regrounded in the depths of human experience and the midst of historical life. They wanted an eschatology grander and more worthy of hope than even Bunyan had offered. Their attempts to rethink eschatology, however, remained at a level of such abstraction that it was not clear how to preach these at funerals, nor how to integrate these into actual dying and death. This left Christian reflection on personal death in a kind of theological backwater, so that on occasions when something *had* to be said, it was spoken without connection to newer visions of eschatology and God's hope. Indeed, since so little was said on the topic, older and less official variants could persist at a popular level, as in the *South Philadelphia Review-Chronicle*'s perpetuation of the nineteenth century's bucolic familial Heaven.

The result of this situation is a temporary vacuum. The death awareness movement emerged within this at first as one more voice against any concern with the eschatological dimensions of death. In its origins, the death awareness movement was unconcerned with life after death. The death awareness movement focused on impending loss, on the naturalness of death, on mourning the loss among those who survived. It bracketed or dismissed what seemed to lie beyond these parameters. The quick verdict of Kübler-Ross in *On Death and Dying* that belief in an afterlife was denial could be balanced only by her qualification that unlike society's blanket denial of death, the religious denial "offered hope and purpose," and gave suffering some meaning. The decline in religious belief in life after death "has been a poor exchange,"[3] but no more development of this topic was part of Kübler-Ross's agenda.

This verdict was representative of the beginning phase of the death awareness movement. Lack of interest in the positive claims of religion and its potential effects on the dying went together with commitment to explore the psychological states of patients. Insofar as the original death awareness movement may have wanted to present itself as scientific thanatology, there was pressure to ignore explicitly old-fashioned religious claims and perspectives. Weisman's phrase, "the future as an illusion," harks backs to Freud's popular attack on religion: "What death means . . . is that the future does not exist."[4] Had the death awareness movement continued to be scientific thanatology, this tone could have been maintained, and the movement's impact and influence would have been a different story. Indeed, it would not have been a "movement" at all.

But this is not what happened. Far from remaining militantly secular, if it ever really was, the death awareness movement developed its own indigenous ethos that now can be called its spirituality. When chaplains, pastoral counselors, and ordinary pastors absorbed the motifs and images of the new approaches, they did so without feeling that their own Christian commitments were being attacked. To read Kübler-Ross was not like reading Freud, for her negative remarks about religious denial played such a minor role in the overall presentation as to be easily discounted. Moreover, chaplains and other Christian counselors drew upon the ideas of the death awareness movement without facing the kind of culture wars that erupted when controversial therapies (e.g., sensitivity groups) were introduced. The many books written to present the five stages of dying and other death awareness motifs as resources for clergy recognized that this material departed from traditional concerns, but authors left these concerns passively bracketed instead of actively undermining them.

The indigenous spirituality of the death awareness movement is naturalist insofar as it discovers transcendence and depth and sacrality within the cycles of natural life and its implicit vision of ecological unity and harmony. Within this imagery, a nonembodied existence outside time and nature would be a superfluity, an excess that would not fit. The real drama, the real quest for divine presence and meaning, would occur prior to death and be focused on acceptance and assent to nature's rhythms. So, when death is a natural event, there is still enough space for ultimacy, for beauty and harmony, for a peace that goes beyond mere rational understanding. When this message is proclaimed and preferred to a message focused on arrival at an afterlife, it seems a mistake to say that the choice is between a secular and a religious view, or between a natural and a spiritual one. For many of us, the Heaven in which Grandma and Pop-pop celebrate their thirtieth anniversary is too small and lacking in transcendence. Its analogic imagination is too constricted to meet the challenge of serious attention to death as the death awareness movement provides. The vision of nature as occasionally glimpsed in the death and dying literature is far more open to ultimacy, to a sense of wonder and paradox, and thus, far more appropriate to the subject itself.

II.

The disappearance of afterlife concerns and imagery in the contemporary death awareness literature and movement needs to be demonstrated rather than simply asserted. Of course, works by psychiatrists such as Weisman will not be focused on this. But how about the patients' own visions of what will happen to them? What of the many first person narratives that chart the illness and the preparations for death from the perspective of the loving caretaker or family member? Autobiographical literature is where the actual concerns of the dying and their survivors overcome any reluctance that scientific thanatology might feel in tackling such metaphysical or religious concerns. Do contemporary death and dying autobiographies come closer to the psychological naturalistic spirituality of the death awareness movement, or to the cosy piety of the *South Philadelphia Review-Chronicle* obituaries and memorials?

The answer to this question is a decisive choice away from eschatology, even among those writers whose religious commitments are beyond doubt. JoAnn Kelley Smith's *Free Fall* (1975) is an early one of these.[5] Smith had lived in intentional Christian communities that practiced care for others, including raising foster children and many other acts of hospitality. When she learns that she will die of cancer, she trusts God to support her even in her "free fall." She resolves to go public and talk with many persons to let them know what the experience of cancer is like, and how struggle with terminal illness can nevertheless be a hopeful time. Like Samson who found honey from a dead lion's corpse, she sees that her quest is for something sweet and satisfying, drawn surprisingly from what is dead and empty. Her major fear is that she will fail to be a "good witness" for Christ, that she may collapse emotionally or become incapacitated by fear and uncertainty.[6] She eventually recognizes that she needs to let go of this ideal. God will accept her pain, her weakness, her imperfections. Thus, she paradoxically becomes a truly good witness for trust in God and acceptance. Smith's book may be no literary masterpiece, but it profoundly links the themes and language of the death awareness movement with Christian concerns. Does Smith believe in heaven? Probably not a South Philadelphia style of heaven, and her struggles are never concerned with any destiny or destination after death. That is not her issue.

Let's take another example of a Christian writer struggling with terminal illness. The author is David Watson, an English evangelist who became active in the charismatic movement. He believes firmly that God can heal, and that it is wrong to be fatalistic about illness and suffering. One should pray against disease, pray for healing, and keep on praying. In *Fear No Evil* he tells how he developed liver cancer, how he and his friends and family responded to this with love, support, and prayer, and how his cancer continued to progress.[7] The struggle here is between his firm hope in God's healing power and his even more basic trust that God is loving and will not be defeated by evil. Watson does not abandon or reject his theology of healing, but he moves past his own expectations and into a more trusting dependence on God. The God he trusts is one whose love he does not pretend to predict or understand, but whose love is certain under all conditions and with all possible outcomes. Obviously aware that some believers in divine healing may conclude from his story that prayer for healing is wrong, he writes in part to reconcile them to a new, more expanded understanding of how God is present even when outcomes are not what we desire. His specific issue is different from JoAnn Kelley Smith's, but the two share a profound wish to explore the experience of cancer and to link what they learned through it to Christian faith. Watson accepted traditional teachings about the afterlife, but these are simply absent from his story.

The deeper the impact of the death awareness movement upon how individuals interpreted their losses and prepared for their own deaths, the more a positive sense of the sacred emerges, intermingling with the daily, dreadful struggles. Imagery from nature is made to bear the weight of awe and meaning in the face of death. No recourse to an after-death existence becomes desirable. In some of the very best contemporary autobiographies, images from nature abound, and are used in striking and significant ways to signify transcendence without afterlife. Terry Tempest Williams's *Refuge* tells the story of her mother's death from breast cancer alongside the story of the flooding of Utah's Great Salt Lake.[8] Williams uses the natural imagery so successfully in part because she is a full-time naturalist, whose understanding and love for the desert milieu is matched by real knowledge of it. The lake's flooding is part of a

larger, more primordial cycle that humans cannot realistically control. Rising water drowns the birds in Williams' favorite bird sanc-
tuary, during the same years that her grandmother and mother both
die of cancer. Eventually the lake recedes and the birds return. The
family deaths, although tragic and disruptive from any other perspective, somehow are made to appear as part of the larger vision
of life and its renewal. Within this overall vision, it is important that
the family is Mormon; they share a history, a practical piety, and a
love of Utah. They do not, however, seem to share the Mormon
hope for families reunited forever in the afterlife. Williams ignores
that level of belief altogether. Once again, afterlife lies outside the
author's story. It is eclipsed by other images and issues. The eschatology that matters is the return of life and birds to the refuge by
the lake, not the return of souls to an eternal realm.

Another successful example of this comes from an autobiographical account whose main purpose is to depict the adventures
of a Westerner in Japan. I include the deathbed scene from Cathy
Davidson's *36 Views of Mt. Fuji* here because it does so well what
other contemporary narratives also often attempt: to present the actual moment of dying as a "sacred time," an event with transcendent implications, yet without any anticipation of an eternal
destination for the dead. In contrast to the Japanese, Davidson
writes, North Americans like her husband's family must create
their own sacred space for death. As her husband's mother lies dying in a hospital in Canada, the family surrounds her. The mix of
"nine different ethnic groups and five different religious back-
grounds, all in one room,"[9] is a matter of pride for her; it is a true
Canadian mosaic, and also means that no one traditional belief can
be shared by all. Yet, when sunset comes, the Native American
member of the family takes on the role of mediating the sacred in
nature. An eagle soars on the horizon. "Grandma, the eagle is
here," he says. She dies.[10] The eagle is not literally believed to be
a messenger from the spirit realm; it is present as an image of transcendence, grandeur, and departure. As such, it requires no distinct
theological commitment. The Roman Catholicism of the dying
mother-in-law plays no role in the death scene, while the Native

American's traditional link with nature gives him the privilege of the last word. This is nature, but not despirited nature. The moment of death is a sacred space, but not a transition into a new, clearly imagined celestial realm.

These four cases deal with the deaths of traditionally religious persons, and one might expect that some imagery from the afterlife would play a role in how they anticipate and prepare for death. Such ideas could have appeared somewhere in the story without feeling like an intrusion of religious propaganda into an otherwise authentic personal narrative. But the afterlife does not appear; lakes and eagles replace it. Therefore, it is hardly surprising that narratives by self-declared nonreligious persons also omit all references to what happens after death and concentrate upon issues of acceptance and letting go, of family ties and natural harmonies. A few define their task as showing how a resolutely secular humanistic attitude toward death can be maintained, but the majority do not need to state that they are nonreligious. The preoccupations of the narratives include the motifs and images of the death awareness movement. What is missing are all references to an afterlife.

Still more curious and convincing evidence of this absence is the same pattern in autobiographies focused on dying and grief written by Westerners who are Buddhists. Traditional Buddhism in East Asia includes a variety of ideas about personal eschatology. Reincarnation, becoming an ancestor, and existence in Amida's Western Paradise have all been possibilities for Japanese Buddhists, for instance; Davidson deliberately introduces the *bon-odori* festival of welcome for the ancestors to contrast with the lack of such traditions in North America. Do personal narratives of illness, dying, and grief written by Western Buddhists include any more references to after-death existence than those of Smith, Watson, and Williams? Do persons become Buddhists in order to seek out better beliefs and images of the afterlife, better, that is, than the picture of the South Philadelphians' heavenly anniversaries?

The answer to this question is a resounding no. Not only do American Buddhists who have participated in the death awareness movement, such as Stephen Levine, focus away from any claims of personal survival after death, but their personal narratives focus on exactly those themes that preoccupy other contemporary North American autobiographers. Buddhists in the West tell stories of grief and bereavement that use natural imagery,[11] or that struggle with grief through an attempt at detachment, at seeing through one's pain to its source—craving or desire. In *Hard Travel to Sacred Places,* author Rudolph Wurlitzer and his wife travel on a photography assignment to Southeast Asia, while still intensely grieving the sudden death of her son.[12] They know the "correct" Buddhist responses to life's sufferings, and the traditional teaching that death's inevitability is a prod to seek the cure to desire. They nevertheless suffer acutely all the way through Thailand, Burma, and war-torn Cambodia. They are, in one sense, struggling just as Smith did with the pressure to be and remain a good witness to a religious faith, while the realities of the situation explode around them. They and other American Buddhists may perform rituals whose original meanings include or center upon the eschatological destiny of the soul of the deceased. But they do so without appropriating those traditional beliefs, and instead present a Buddhism in which reincarnation and other destinies just do not appear, and would be labelled delusion by the authors if they did appear. Eschatology is eclipsed in Christians' autobiographies, and it is eclipsed in these Buddhist narratives along the same lines.

III.

The most remarkable fact is not this eclipse of eschatology in the death awareness literature's psychological models and in contemporary personal narratives, but its reappearance in a separate area that lies outside the mainstream of the death awareness movement. I refer to the topic or genre of near-death experiences (NDEs) that took flight after the publication in 1976 of Raymond Moody's *Life after Life.* This publicized radically different imagery for dying and death than anything examined so far. Moody's book laid out a schema for the NDE[13] that other authors have either

further elaborated or bolstered by adding new testimonies following the original Moody model. A secondary literature about such
experiences or about the narratives that present them now exists.
It is fascinating how completely this topic has remained a separate
track, with imagery and a message distinct from the death awareness movement's focus on natural event and loss. That it seems to
escape from the general disinterest in afterlife and eschatology is
astonishing, but its substantive overall contribution of new words
for dying and death is still controversial. To some extent, its popularity may rest on the same stratum of nineteenth-century heritage
that the obituaries of the *South Philadelphia Review-Chronicle* reveal, although its advocates are often assumed to be New Agers,
more interested in the future and its promise than in the past.

Moody's *Life after Life* starts from the claim that those who
come close to death but "return" have stories to tell, stories that
dramatically contradict the mainstream, naturalistic views of death
as an ending. Instead, death appears as transition to a transfigured,
beautiful, peaceful realm. This transition is imaged as travel
through a dark tunnel, with a bright light at the end. The soul who
makes this journey has left its body lying on the operating table or
in the wrecked car, and is able to move into an otherworld where
it meets a Being of Light. This Being is loving, not frightening.
The most common interaction is a life-review, where the soul is
shown its own history, although this is not to be confused with a
judgment in the traditional sense. Some of the travellers enter a
beautiful realm of transfigured colors, where they meet their own
beloved dead. But they are always sent back; it is not yet their time
to remain in the other place. They awake, and for many it is a struggle to return psychologically to the world they were very willing
to leave in their visions. All of them report that life after death is
now a reality; they no longer believe, they *know*. Hence, they no
longer have any fear of dying.

Do these tales constitute proof of a life after life? In the introduction to a recent anthology, *The Near-Death Experience,* editors
Lee Bailey and Jenny Yates believe this to be the primary significance of these phenomena.

> What is the Big Secret? What experience lies waiting behind the
> curtain when we die? Does consciousness disappear—poof!—
> into an empty void because it is a by-product of the physical
> body that no longer functions? . . . Or does the soul lift grace-
> fully about the physical world into a majestic, incredibly beau-
> tiful realm full of love and joy, our true home before and after
> this brief incarnation? The answer to *that* is the Big Secret.[14]

This is exactly the issue missing from the death awareness movement and from the range of autobiographies just discussed. It is the
classic, traditional question of survival after death, and only the
NDE literature treats it as central. Most advocates, critics, and
commentators have wanted answers to this "Big Secret." Failure
to find one that unequivocally convinces all parties has led to a
kind of impasse in debates over NDEs.

It can help to separate the issue of survival after death from that
of body-soul dualism. The NDE accounts divide into those that take
the transition into the "other world," and those in which the disembodied soul or spirit views events in *this* world, all the while seemingly unconscious. From the room's ceiling, the temporarily
evicted soul watches and listens to medical procedures, and even
travels to nearby rooms to observe things and people there. That
some of these sights and sounds can be externally verified afterward makes the whole phenomenon even more mysterious and in-
triguing. Is the real explanation of these NDEs an increase of
endorphins in the brain? If so, how can anyone explain an accurate
observation of a hospital procedure carried out while the patient
was presumably unconscious? Moreover, the whole phenomenon
of out of body experience requires an unmitigated dualism between
body and soul that flies in the face of so much twentieth-century
thinking—scientific, popular, and certainly religious—that its fla-
grant reappearance in these accounts is just one more remarkable
aspect of them.

The debates over these experiences have been sterile in large part
because of scientific defensiveness and reductionism on the part of
those who want to use "endorphins" or some other physiological-
chemical explanation to debunk the entire phenomenon. This re-

sponse, far from being the objective science its partisans claim, is in fact "the conservative reaction . . . to recent social changes, particularly those of postmodernity and science. . . . [T]he skeptics are not attacking, but rather defending."[15] The other problem is that few on either side have understood that NDEs are *narratives,* not the kind of scientific data that can be falsified or validated. When anyone with sensitivity to narrative approaches the same material, the question of proof for survival of physical death gives way to how the imagination constructs a realm of possibilities nonreductively and often with great power. Carol Zaleski's fine historical treatment of NDEs in *Otherworld Journeys* reveals how literalized hopes about the "Big Secret" have remained.[16] Moody's schema fixed, perhaps prematurely and unfortunately, a range of contemporary possibilities to reach beyond "death as natural." Such new words address dimensions of dying that the death awareness movement itself, let alone mainstream contemporary society, had forgotten.

However, anyone who doubts that the death awareness movement and the NDE genre constitute two separate tracks of contemporary imagery should try to immerse herself in the latter after familiarity with the former. The NDE narratives seem to all feed off each other. Most have "the Light" in their titles: *Saved by the Light, Embraced by the Light, Closer to the Light, Transformed by the Light, To Touch the Light, One with the Light.*[17] All include testimonies, some claim the status of scientific research, and others are primarily personal narrative. For instance, Betty Eadie's *Embraced by the Light* is filled with very detailed reports of what she learned in the after-death realm about the destinies of spirits, Adam and Eve, and much else. Dannion Brinkley in *Saved by the Light* receives prophetic information in 1975 from thirteen Beings of Light about political events, including the Gulf War. The longer and more elaborated the NDE accounts become, the more space there is for a variety of agendas (conservative Christian, New Age, political) to be included within them.

Within this genre, death is anything but natural event, and anything but loss. Death is transition, and indeed in some of the phrasing, "death" is omitted altogether (e.g., Moody's *Life after Life*). One makes a transition from this life—the operating table or the car wreck—into the tunnel and out into the other realm, without any imagery of destruction or mutilation. Moreover, the necessary dualism of body and soul (Platonic more than Cartesian, but dualistic throughout) requires that the soul, the travelling consciousness, be the real bearer of identity. The body's fate is that of casing or vessel or vehicle. The sight of one's own ill or unconscious body is disturbing, but for the NDE narrators this is peripheral. To separate from one's container is a liberation toward a new and more glorious life, toward "the Light"; it is not a divorce from what ties us most into biological nature and its rhythms.

Even more prominently in this literature, death is never a loss. In the words of one case history, "She wanted them to understand that death was nothing to fear. Dying might be a horrible experience, but once that was over, death itself was wonderful."[18] Everything that the death awareness movement says about dying is relativized, because if death itself is wonderful then dying can be a transition whose unpleasantness is not worth dwelling upon. It is sure to be forgotten once the wonderful goal is reached. All of the autobiographers discussed in the previous section resist this message with all their strength. For them, dying is what is happening now, it is where God can work, it is where nature's power and sacrality can emerge. It is not something horrible to be "gotten through" and devalued, even if at the end there is something wonderful awaiting all of us. I believe even John Bunyan, whose views might easily lend themselves to a "dying is horrible, death is wonderful" position, would have drawn a different conclusion than the *Light* books. The road along the way to the Celestial City matters; it is dangerous and filled with treacherous and difficult adventures, but it is not without meaning. The final river crossing is an important consummating test, not just a horrible experience.

Elisabeth Kübler-Ross herself embraced the Light, or at least wholeheartedly adopted the view now described. In *On Children and Death,* published in 1983, she tries to join this view of transition into a new and improved spiritual existence, with her original model of five stages focused on coming to terms with loss. The result is a disturbing mishmash, for the families and children who struggle with denial and anger give way to other narratives of children drawn into a world of Light prior to their deaths. In this landscape death as ending no longer exists. Death is just like a caterpillar becoming a butterfly,[19] it is a transformation that Kübler-Ross and others who use it today do not construe as a loss. Unlike St. Teresa of Avila, who used this same image (the silkworm) to describe the mystical "death" of the soul prior to the highest levels of union with God, there is no room for death at all in the way this metamorphosis is imagined. Is it still a natural event? Yes and no. Caterpillars become butterflies as part of their life cycle, and in that sense the imagery from nature can serve to familiarize this view. But the thrust of the NDE view yanks humans out of natural rhythms, restores our Platonic transcendence. Our disembodied "real" identity discards the body.

Supposing that death is a gain and not a loss from the perspective of the near-death experiencer, what of the survivors around that person? Another curious feature of the NDE genre is how lightly this question is treated. Recall that for the death awareness movement, although one's own death has frequently but not universally been construed as an impending loss, there was never a doubt that this same death was a loss for others. Bereavement and the tasks or processes of mourning are taken so seriously by the death awareness movement that its advocates protest any attempt to minimize or deny the reality of loss from this point of view. The *Light* books almost all ignore this concern. The NDE protagonist encounters the Being of Light, and is ready to enter the realm that lies beyond. What about children and other dependents? What will become of them? How will the protagonist's death affect them? When this concern is mentioned, which in the majority of popular writings it is not, the answer appears to be a glib, "They'll get over it." Of course, these people all did return from their experiences. They are writing their narratives knowing that they did in fact return to earth and its relationships. They want to stress how compellingly real and attractive the other realm was, not how important were the bonds that tied them to life. Just as caterpillar into butterfly imagery looks a lot like denial from the stance of the death awareness movement, so this disappearance of survivors' loss looks peculiar. Indeed, it appears a lot like one more piece of disenfranchised grief, of denial that something really sad has happened to someone.

IV.

Two tracks seem to be what now exist. There are almost no Moody-type experiences in the death and dying autobiographies; there is a blocking off of concern with death as loss in the *Light* genre. Superficially, the latter comes closer to traditional Christian theological territory, for its "Big Secret" seems to replicate the association between religion and personal afterlife. The death awareness movement appears unable or uninterested in assimilating the NDE genre, or at least in adopting its primary images and messages.

Maggie Callanan and Patricia Kelley's *Final Gifts: Understanding the Special Awareness, Needs and Communications of the Dying* is an unusually successful attempt to intermingle these "two tracks." This 1992 best-seller takes the down-to-earth credibility of the death awareness movement's literature with the topics that reach into the NDE genre, thereby showing that the two tracks can potentially be reconciled.

The authors, two hospice nurses, not only appear credible to those familiar with hospice, but present case histories that read like other stories of dying persons, including those from many of the autobiographies. They have a stake in promoting peaceful dying, but they avoid claims that "death is wonderful." The dying people they have observed actually behave like people with little physical energy to spend on elaborate communications of something that may well be indescribable anyway. The authors insist that the dying are engaged in special symbolic communications when to the outward eye all that appears is confusion. The dying also can have some control over the timing of their own deaths, so that they can alert family members in advance that their death is near. On these matters, Callanan and Kelley remain well within the framework of the mainstream death awareness movement, offering insights and observations without attempting medical-scientific explanations.

But the same authors embrace elements of the NDE literature, especially the metaphor of a journey and presence of the beloved dead at the deathbed. They insist that the dying do not have to leave their bodies or fly through tunnels to see those whom to all others remain invisible.[20] Nevertheless, the imagery of travel seems to fit. Travel is obviously a metaphor here[21] and even the naturalistic early Kübler-Ross found the patients themselves speak of their impending deaths this way.[22] But in Callanan and Kelley it becomes something more, for "seeing a place" is included as one of the experiences frequently reported by those near death.

> Many dying people tell of seeing a place not visible to anyone else. Their descriptions are brief—rarely exceeding a sentence or two—and not very specific, but usually glowing. . . . [T]he response to "Tell me more . . . " often is a dreamy look and a shake of the head or several false starts and then "I can't."[23]

The authors insist that "a glimpse of this other place seems to bring peace, comfort and security" to both the dying and those able to listen and understand. This is travel and a destination. The details are few, and correspond with some of the Moody-type basics: light, beauty, peace. For the authors, this suggests its experiential if not metaphysical reality; as the dying "drift in and out of the other place, they assure us of its existence, its beauty, and its peace."[24]

Another NDE phenomenon appears, albeit in unsensationalized and subdued form: the dying person sees and recognizes the beloved dead and/or spiritual beings, who accompany him or her into the realm beyond. The authors advise:

> The most important thing to remember when a dying person sees someone invisible to you is that death is not lonely. . . . In fact, what the stories of these people tell us is that they didn't die alone, and neither will we. Those who have died before us, or some spiritual beings, will be companions on our journey.[25]

Death is not lonely, because someone will be there with us. The spirits of the dead are seen—by the dying person alone—hovering above the bed. None of the exorbitantly exotic details of the *Light* books are here because the authors maintain that in the case of gradually dying persons rather than traumatic near-deaths, the whole tenor of the experience shifts.

Is this a difference in two types of experiences and situations? Partly this is a difference in authors' intentions and publishers' marketing strategies. Callanan and Kelley do whatever they can to normalize and domesticate the eerie experience of a boundary permeable, of a landscape between the earth of this world and the ocean of another. Even the cover of their book is pale-colored, showing a low-key photo of an empty chair facing an open window, in great contrast to the exorbitantly "supernatural" splashy marketing of the *Light* genre. About that other realm, not much can be said, and so *Final Gifts* remains in continuity with autobiographies such as those by Williams and Davidson. That other place and its inhabitants are acknowledged to be present in this world at the edges. This is handled in a way that the death awareness advocates can honor rather than find suspect.

Callanan and Kelley show how the death awareness movement may revise the "Big Secret" of the NDE genre and its critics. As both sides of that debate by now recognize, it is not possible to jump from experience of life at the edge of death into rationally grounded claims about a reality *after* death. Thus, the sterility of the conflicting explanations of the NDE will continue so long as the "Big Secret" is at stake. What happens in *Final Gifts,* however, is that a pervasive view of dying as the most solitary and isolating act of a human is challenged at a level hard to discount entirely. To a large extent, the death awareness movement has assumed the fundamental solitariness of death, even while trying to alleviate its depressing intensification within the hospital. The death awareness movement has accepted the Ivan Ilych model where individual dying is intensely private because the ultimate authentic self is uniquely atomistic and alone. The claim made here by Callanan and Kelley is that this is wrong. It is not just incomplete but fundamentally off-base.

Recall the presence of Christ on the cross for the dying of the *Ars Moriendi* literature. Here, too, we found the loving assurance that "you will not die alone," although the important specifics of the eschatologies are different. In turn, this assurance harks back to Jesus' own words of promise: "In my Father's house are many rooms. . . . I am going there to prepare a place for you. . . . I will come back and take you to be with me that you also may be where I am" (John 14:2–3). From within the death awareness movement itself this cannot be said directly, but the movement's earlier most prevalent assumptions are now open to challenge from within. Perhaps from the stance of the death awareness advocates, so firmly planted in hospitals, hospices, and other health care environments of this world, this is enough. Any credible and authentic eschatology will be restricted to this quiet secret presence of the dead alongside the dying. Like the eagle in Davidson's story, it signifies what exists just beyond our earth, in the sacred space that contemporary dying has discovered and about which it will speak so tentatively and metaphorically when it speaks well.

V.

I have tried in this discussion to avoid predetermined battle lines, such as have already been set by confrontations between New Age spiritualities and those who identify themselves as spokespersons for "authentic" Christianity. This battle is even more sterile, I believe, than the battle over the "Big Secret" that has been the focus of the NDE literature. The boundaries of Christian imagery and teachings regarding death have been more open to change than some Christians have recognized. On this basis alone, if the death awareness movement has something to contribute, even supplementally, then Christians ought to be informed and feel free to borrow and adapt its contributions. On the other hand, one must be aware of the limits both of newer contributions and some of the older alternatives. I have shown at what points there is conflict as well as complementarity in the death awareness movement's perspective.

The NDE material, on the other hand, is another story. It is not only New Age in its vocabulary, it is blatantly eschatological yet also directly incompatible with some doctrines that have mattered and continue to matter to many Christians. On this ground, it has been the target of innumerable attacks. Some claim that NDE experiences of the Moody type must be demonically inspired, precisely because they so closely counterfeit the real claims of Christianity while simultaneously undermining these. According to this argument, the NDE genre is suspect for its blanket lack of interest in salvation through Christ, its universalism, and its nonjudgmental Being of Light who may be Christ but need not be. Those who take this approach go directly to theological criteria of Christian doctrines. A problem with this line of argument is that it could just as easily be turned against the heavenly anniversaries of the *South Philadelphia Review-Chronicle,* as indeed such arguments were launched against Elizabeth Phelps and her heavenly landscape. Perhaps the real reason such a battle has not been waged is that the authors of the letters to "Mom and Pop in Heaven" do not have the cultural influence today, while the New Age spokespersons are perceived as culturally triumphant.

New Agers seem to enjoy this kind of criticism, and have gleefully repeated it as proof of the close-mindedness and backward-looking outlook of Christians. Curiously, even those narratives of the the *Light* genre whose authors claim to validate Christian doctrines through retelling their NDE seem to provide momentum for the New Age claim to have gone beyond medicine and religion. Why worry about theological categories when one can share personal revelation, receive inside knowledge of what Beings of Light are up to or how "spirit children" are assigned to future parents or when new wars will break out? Christian opponents of the NDE genre point to these examples and conclude that in no way do the *Light* books meet any theological criteria for orthodoxy; indeed, their main effect is to distract us with visions while debunking the need for any reflective criteria whatsoever. Advocates of the *Light* extoll personal experience over any shared standards of religious or rational truths. They happily reply that religious freedom and experimentation are the stuff of the future, the New Age that will hopefully lead us all away from theological rigidity and witch-hunts.

In actuality, this picture of mutual hostility and suspicion between Christians and believers in NDEs over theological vaguaries and errors is quite erroneous. It may fit a conservative Christian polemic against "occult" forces in society, and certainly fits within a New Age polemic against "Old Age" religion, but in this case, the actual spread and meanings of NDEs escape from this conflict. A study by David Royse from the *Journal of Pastoral Care* showed that Christian clergy were far from negative or ill-disposed toward the subject.[26] Seventy-one percent had heard NDE accounts from their parishoners, or were approached to discuss the topic. Three-quarters of those surveyed felt it was appropriate or at least unproblematic to discuss this with the dying. Clergy were in no way the enemies of personal religious experience, nor was their primary interest to impose theological tests to invalidate what persons they spoke with wanted to share. In other words, the actual reception of these NDE stories reveals very little of the well-publicized conflict between "counterfeit spirituality" and New Age advocacy. Perhaps one reason why little evidence of sharp conflict appears here is that the clergy were far more likely to have heard stories such as those in *Final Gifts* than anything like what gets published in the *Light* books. As we have seen, the near death awareness depicted by Callanan and Kelley is shorn of those features that make the Moody-type of NDE the target of vigorous attack.

But shouldn't Christians be a bit more on guard when faced with *Saved by the Light, Embraced by the Light,* and all their sensational and death-defying, death-denying messages? To note the death awareness movement's original absence of eschatology, is not to promote the thesis that any reappearance of afterlife concerns is good thing and ought to be welcomed. I can document a real gap, a real "eclipse," just as in the case of the justice and punishment imagery for death, but I remain convinced that to fill in this absence with the stuff of the *Light* books is to do a real disservice. As Christians, we are obligated to historical theological norms, not as straightjackets to impede experience, but as guides and frameworks to help construct and meaningfully interpret experiences. Moreover, those who do not take Christian truth as authoritative will not become free of authorities. They will instead be overwhelmed by such authorities as advertisers, supermarket tabloids, talk show hosts, anyone whose fifteen minutes of fame is gained by claims about revelations of life after death. Christians not only have a responsibility to identify and resist the use of such "authorities," but to contribute to our society's fragile yet emergent ability to say something real about dying and loss. A genuine Christian spirituality of dying and death and grief leaves room for near-death experience, but not for the message that dying is horrible but death itself is wonderful. At least not as this message is heard here and now, as it plays into a society still caught in the effects of "wild death," of denial and silence. NDE happens; it is real in that sense. But how to make sense of it, to sort through its images to avoid those that only support denial, remains a challenge. No message that negates the reality of loss, that avoids rather than encompasses pain, can really work in the long run.

On the other hand, what the NDE authors call the "Big Secret" is not, for Christians, really secret at all. Not since Jesus' own resurrection from death has the image of death as complete negation and extinction been appropriate. How to express this via the religious imagination, without literalizing our intimations, sensationalizing them, or using them in the service of denial, is a difficult task. The death awareness movement, while initially eclipsing eschatology as a formal area of interest, is now prepared to step beyond that. Perhaps its real impact may be to reopen Christian thought to this topic, rescuing the whole discussion from its backwater status. To reopen sacred space for dying is now possible, and this takes us beyond the full eclipse of eternity, as well as beyond wild death's silence and denial. Christians need not follow all the way through the *Light* books to rejoice in this change.

MEDITATION 6: JESUS' LAST WORDS
Matthew 27:46; Mark 15:34; Luke 23:46; John 19:30

The ancient church wisely rejected attempts to harmonize the four canonical Gospels. We are presented with a range of three possible last words of Jesus, each of which could only be meaningful as the very last thing he said before his death. Because Mark and Matthew coincide on this point, their version of the last words seems privileged. Jesus cries out, "Eloi, Eloi, lama sabachthani?" translated as "My God, my God, why have you forsaken me?" This is a direct quote from Psalm 22:1, which then seems to have led the Gospel authors or their sources to include details in the story that intentionally evoke and echo other verses of the psalm. Although Matthew's Gospel was traditionally given a privileged place because of its many teaching sections, Mark is preferred almost universally by biblical scholars as the earliest, and therefore most authentic of the four full narratives. However, because no one narrative fully substitutes for all the others, even prior to modern biblical criticism no one could be absolutely certain which last words of Jesus were truly his final saying.

What does it matter? Why do last words have any special significance? The death awareness movement deemphasizes any traditional folk beliefs on this matter, but this is almost surely because in the high-tech hospital setting, patients are too zonked out by pain medications to say much of anything. Even those who insist on "conscious dying" as a goal rarely put very much weight on one's final sayings. Stephen Levine cites Gandhi, who died with the name of God upon his lips, but his aim is to connect this practice with earlier preparation, with a conscious life before dying.[27] Although dying while repeating the name of God may be especially blessed, contemporary death awareness advocates see no link between this practice and an auspicious afterlife. Instead, the significance of last words is that they might serve to sum up a life, and today this is explicitly downplayed. The Callanan and Kelley reports about presences, journeys, and places never give last words in and of themselves any of this weight.

But the four Gospels are carefully crafted narratives, and it is impossible to sever the last words of Jesus from the overall flow and direction of each narrative. From this stance, Jesus' last words matter. The desolate cry of abandonment in both Mark and Matthew is a shocking choice of last words for someone whose whole life was an experience of intimacy with God as his loving Father. Luke's final words have Jesus commit his spirit to his Father, a more fitting ending as a summation of his life and identity, while John's Gospel's declaration, "It is finished!" stresses finality. There is nothing left for Jesus to do now but die. What is important is not just how the narratives tell the story, but how we, readers in the midst of a struggle to say new words for dying and death, read and hear what they have to say. Particularly, how has our own "eclipse of eternity," the absence of afterlife imagery in our own era and in the death awareness movement's mainstream, affected what we can apprehend?

To answer this question, we must remember that the absence of afterlife imagery preceded the death awareness movement and was noticeable in theology in the early twentieth century. This absence also penetrated biblical scholarship, which in fact has been a kind of subfield of theology, at least in Protestant circles. If the afterlife was not a major topic, and became a theological as well as cultural backwater area, then this affected how even those claiming to do objective historical criticism judged the narratives they studied. This bias, shared by so much of the death awareness literature, predisposed many to turn away from references to an afterlife, devalue them, isolate them from what was believed to be the core of what really happened. Attacks on the historicity of the resurrection of Jesus led by Bultmann and others are only the most blatant example of this use of twentieth-century criteria of what is believable.

However, this same predisposition works in favor of Jesus' last words. Not just Matthew's and Mark's cry of abandonment, but even the versions of last words in Luke and John stand up relatively well to this narrowed vision. "It is finished" seems to omit the resurrection, seems to make the cross the consummation and completion of Jesus' mission. No references to a future resurrected existence, to a return back upward to the Father appear in any of these final sayings. Bultmann took this as evidence that an original *kerygma* (gospel proclamation) had not depended upon such a mythological idea as resurrection, and that only a later level of editing or church doctrinal elaboration included this in the story. Not many biblical scholars have gone quite so directly or crudely toward this conclusion, but the lack of transition or resurrection imagery in Jesus' last words is never a problem or a paradox from their point of view. If for us eternity is absent, then what counts as a problem is its appearance, the liberal peppering of references to it in the sayings of Jesus prior to his death as well as the major narratives of his empty tomb and appearances.

Jesus freely uses transition imagery for his death elsewhere in the Gospels. In John, he forewarns his followers of his impending return to the Father (16:5ff; 17:13). As the Word of the prologue, he descends—and now is ready to ascend back to his original home. On the cross, however, he is lifted up not to heaven, but to a publicly displayed death. His last statement is emphatically not about rising, taking a journey, or glimpsing a place beyond this world. This paradoxical appearance of transition imagery elsewhere and its absence in Jesus' last words is even more true for Mark. At the Last Supper, Jesus declares, "I will not drink again of the fruit of the vine until that day when I drink it anew in the kingdom of God" (14:25), which is as clear a use of transition images for his own death as one could ask for. Not only does Jesus predict his death and his resurrection in these narratives, but he offers pictures of a future where he will return gloriously or judge the world as he comes into his kingdom. Luke, as we have seen, has him promise the repentant criminal a place in Paradise, in the final human interchange of his life. And Matthew, eager to anticipate the resurrection, tells how the dead of Jerusalem arose from their tombs and walked the city immediately after Jesus' death (27:52–53). It is as if this imagery appears to surround Jesus' last words on both sides, but never is included within them.

If our bias is to eliminate or eclipse this topic, then the solution is to delegitimate as many of these references as possible from the true core of the narrative. This has been done, not just by Bultmann's scheme of a pre-Gospel that did not rely on resurrection, but much more pervasively by the argument that all of the predictions are fundamentally retroactive interpretations by the early church. According to this understanding, the church accepted the resurrection and reinterpreted everything Jesus did or said in its light, peppering authentic sayings and actions with added references to a future about which no one including Jesus could have known a thing before it happened. Thus, any attempt to argue the resurrection by claims that Jesus predicted it are turned on their head. The predictions only appear post-Easter, they are evidence of how important the resurrection was to the early church, and the narratives must be read this way. Therefore, although an afterlife is not absent, it is made secondary.

Unfortunately, there are two major problems with this strategy. The most obvious one—which Bultmann recognized and tried to overcome—is that it places much more weight on the resurrection as *fact,* as event so decisive that it caused the early church to engage in such energetic and thorough revision of its memories of Jesus. It places more weight than if Jesus had all along been preaching and teaching about the topic, about death as a transition, about his own death as a transition into the kingdom. For those whose eclipse of eternity is expressed in the language of what is scientifically believable, this makes the whole scheme very precarious, for the resurrection is just the kind of "fact" that appears too dubious to bear this weight. The second problem is different, but more relevant to our specific focus. Why, if the early church was so intent on postresurrection additions and reinterpretations, did they stop when it came to Jesus' last words? Why not have him say, "I go now back to the Father" or, "Father, I await your act of victory over death; I pray to enter my kingdom now"? Why limit the reinterpretation, especially at the very point where it might be most plausible and powerful to include it?

I believe the answer is that this was not an issue for the early church or the Gospel authors, but for us in the twentieth century. The absence of resurrection or transition images in all three of Jesus' last sayings strikes us as *realism;* it is stark and naked, and unadorned to us. We are predisposed to find the lack of lights, angels, and journey images more compellingly close to what we think we know of dying. It is Stephen's death in Acts 7 which includes this kind of material that seems fanciful—although by the standards of the *Light* books it is quite tame. So we come to Jesus' last words and find, with relief, no need to demythologize them, to strip them of imagery we do not understand.

This is particularly true of the forsaken cry of despair in Mark and Matthew. This one feels real. It is filled with horror. Jesus dies alone, with no awareness of God's presence. No matter how Callanan and Kelley try to assure us, Jesus here experienced nothing of death's light and peace and companionship. Far more than the death awareness movement, this cry permits the presence of wild death in the midst of the Gospel, an ultimate negativity and ending and isolation. This has been rediscovered in our century because it echoes our own imagery of death as unimaginable and final and completely destructive. Jesus seems to us to bear the full weight of what we, still locked into wild death, really believe death to be about. To the extent that the death awareness movement throws its own weight into a battle against denial and silence, it will recognize that facing death means coming to grasp this dimension of its reality. It can thereby share this appropriation of Jesus' final words and their meaning. When all attention is turned toward death as natural, as somehow comfortable, death awareness advocates will not be able to encompass this message.

Perhaps it is not the death awareness movement's sharing in the eclipse of eternity, but its way to overcome silence and denial with new words that perpetuates the problem. In the end its new images do not seem equal to this expression of abandonment and despair. It cannot express how Jesus' dying words introduce death into God and bring a sense of separation and loss right into the Trinity. Perhaps it never intends to say this much directly about theological topics. Perhaps even the biblical scholars and theologians are reading the narratives so selectively that death's terror stands in artificial isolation away from all the imagery of transition into eternal life found within the same texts. Yet we who are Christians can choose among three possible last words of Jesus, but cannot chose to depart from all three. To remain faithful to Jesus in his dying and to anticipate our own faithfully, we need to hear what he said and to trust that this will truthfully guide our own imagery for dying and death.

Conclusion

Christians and the Death Awareness Movement

This work has surveyed some of the central images and ideas of the new words for dying and death that have been spoken over the last thirty years. Insofar as these have taken us beyond silence, denial, and the era of "wild death," then all of us, Christians and others, benefit from the death awareness movement. Saying *something* about such topics as death and grief is better than remaining without words or images, caught in the grip of death's presence yet without either others' words from the past or words of our own. In this book I have tried to make clear why some words are better than others, some images more fitting than others, from a Christian perspective.

Christians have not started from the baseline of "death is natural," but this does not mean that such a claim is anti-Christian. Within the context of high-tech hospitals and medicalized death, which is the setting for this claim, the push to move beyond medicine's "war against death at all cost" is an important and humane agenda. One wishes, however, that an alternative could be found to "natural" even within this setting. Death as "appropriate," as "acceptable"—an anticipated if not desirable end to the life cycle—is not the final word Christians should say on death, but under contemporary conditions it is a start. Christians also affirm both that death is part of God's plan, and that nothing, including dying and death, can separate us from communion with God. These affirmations offer effective and fundamental defenses against the isolation and loss of moral authority that is so much a part of medicalized death.

In contrast, death as loss is a different matter, for it covers territory not specifically treated in Christian thinking. As we saw in the way funeral liturgies have subtly shifted to make room for this motif, there is space for death as loss if Christians recognize this as only one of several images for death. Death is a loss from both the perspective of the dying and that of the mourners. This idea is a useful supplement to Christian eschatological hope. The choice is not between mourning *or* resurrection, sorrow *or* joy, Good Friday *or* Easter. Christian faith is complex, rich and realistic enough to encompass all of these dimensions. I am sure that Christians intuitively recognize this, yet I believe it needs to be affirmed clearly. If there is a time to mourn, there is also a time to rejoice. Once we leave silence and denial behind, Christians can integrate the best approaches of the death awareness movement into pastoral practice, without losing sight of other images that also belong to the landscape of faith.

Moreover, Christians ought to support recognition of grief. Disenfranchised grief is a heavy burden, a genuine problem that Christians together should identity and confront. Pressures to return to work, to "get on with life," to ignore the inner and interpersonal work of mourning, are so great today that the church should identify and resist these, offering an alternative vision and a space to be bereaved.

The death awareness movement's principal gaps and omissions are those of our society: a sense of judgment and promise of eternity are missing or in eclipse. These missing elements should be filled by Christians from the resources of our traditions. We may no longer like to hear "death is a punishment for sin," but Christians need to recognize a moral framework that includes God's justice, God's judgment over our actions, and God's willingness to forgive our sins. The other area where new words do not cover what was once so important, is eschatology. Today the absence of afterlife concerns is so dramatic and so different from the past that some Christians abandon all attention to "after" and concentrate on transcendence within this life. Then "surviving death" becomes a matter only for mourners, as it is in much of the death awareness literature. But this is a mistake, because it closes off the Christian witness to death's meanings and to God's promise to bring us eternal life beyond death. Jesus went before us to prepare a place with him, and we may trust that we will be with him. We are hidden in Christ both now and after our deaths.

The answer here is that death as mystery is both ending and transition. Death awareness authors struggle, sometimes clumsily, to make this apparent. Motifs of journey, of encounters with the recently dead and so on, are not just New Age propaganda; these appear in the spontaneous narratives of contemporary persons. Something about dying moves one into a place where boundaries become fluid, where movement and travel rather than only finality are the important images to use. To admit this is to be far less literalistic than the *Light* books, of course. But it remains open to an imagery of dying as a sacred time, in a manner that supplements if not reverses some of the message of "death is natural." If this is what the death awareness movement can offer, we as Christians cannot use its contribution to debunk all traces of eschatological thinking. We cannot say that the death awareness movement proves that death is really and completely extinction, solely a natural ending. The more open we are to what the dying are really saying, the less we should foreclose on reality, or rule out what does not automatically make sense to us. As Christians, we may trust, if we listen both to the Gospel narratives and contemporary testimonies, that this will be a much more nuanced and profound message than that of the *Light* books' "Dying is a horrible experience, but death itself is wonderful."

In this book, I present Christianity as a relatively static, bounded collection of doctrines and images, focused on traditional thinking about Jesus's death, salvation, and eternal life. For some persons, this is itself a problem. They would ask, "Why shouldn't Christianity become more fluid and tolerant? Why must it remain so fixated on particular stories and ideas?" According to this view, Christians should be able to accomodate concern with creation rather than redemption, able to make room for pantheistic or panentheistic (God as present fully within the natural world, but not equated with it) imagery, as well as varieties of images for transformation that do not focus upon a personal savior. Maybe the future Christian perspective on death will find an image of the Divine Spirit flowing through all things and connecting all life and levels of reality more compelling and meaningful than the death imagery from the passion story. Just as the social boundaries between Christian and non-Christian may no longer be so important in an era of deinstitutionalized spirituality, so these shifts ought to be accommodated, and I should let go of my portrait of Christian faith centered upon certain specific figures, ideas, images.

To this argument I reply that pleas for diversity and fluidity work best when all involved know the teachings and images from the past, and can therefore say in an informed way what these teachings lack. Today, thanks in part to "wild death," this is no longer the case. The young seminarian who assumed that "Death is natural" was *all* there was to say needed to learn that a lot more has and should be said. His claim revealed ignorance, not a respect for diversity. Given these conditions, a book such as this that abides by traditional boundaries, images, and motifs is more helpful than it is exclusionary. An important educational goal is better awareness that Christian reflection on dying, death, afterlife, and related themes has more to offer than the literalized Heaven of the *South Philadelphia Review-Chronicle* memorials.

However, in order to pursue that goal in this book, I more or less sever a Christian approach to dying and death from other doctrines and teachings that might restore some balance and connection to other areas of concern. It is not Christianity that isolates death from life, but contemporary society. A more classical Christian focus links holy dying to holy living, and doctrines of the Holy Spirit and the Spirit's work in our lives (sanctification) ought to address both. What traditional pastor spent *all* his time with the dying and bereaved? Very few, while today the death awareness movement has, perhaps against its original intentions, expanded specialism into care for the dying and bereaved. But why not challenge specialism and its consequences by returning to a more comprehensive vision of Christian life? This includes a retrieval of Christian doctrines beyond those directly relevant to death. For example, theologically informed Christians argue that the best antidote against the individualism of many psychologically based models of persons is a grasp of the church as Christ's body and as a community of faith. When we understand these ideas of Christian community, we will not be persuaded by death awareness movement personality theories that are thoroughly nonrelational, and exclusively concerned with individual "growth." Those who neglect traditional theological categories and concerns lose an important resource to reconnect death and life.

Another set of connections may be obscured as well by isolating dying, death, and grief from other topics. A resurgence of interest in Christian spiritual practice, in mysticism as a living possibility of deep relationship with God, is part of the contemporary landscape of faith. Christians enthusiastically attend workshops on contemplative prayer, receive spiritual direction, and read the writings of Teresa of Avila, Julian of Norwich, and many other figures. De-monasticizing many of these traditional materials is challenge enough. (Although many spiritual classics were written explicitly for those in ordinary secular life, the majority seem to have presupposed a special religious vocation in an intentional community.) But how to link the advice and piety built upon self-denial, sacrifice, hierarchy, and obedience to duty with our own lives and needs is an ongoing negotiation between the texts and ourselves.

One of the chief discoveries for all who pick up such writings is that "death" for Christian spirituality has never been exclusively the physical death and dying of scientific medicine or thanatology. Death is pervasive imagery, linked to Christ's death, to our own sacrifice of self, to a life "hid with Christ in God." Death in this context is so central a part of Christian piety and devotion that to chart its appearance and applications would be a monumental task.

To expand our contemporary, necessary yet relatively narrow and medicalized focus on terminally ill hospital patients with the rich and symbolic possibilities of the spiritual writers' death imagery, is one important step to reconnect a focus on Christian death with a wider vision of death in the midst of life. To recover this symbolism, to learn to use it in ways that do not trivialize or literalize it, is a vital aspect of the rediscovery of spirituality and traditional spiritual writings.

I believe this new appropriation of death-imagery can help us overcome medicalization even if not at the level of programs or institutions. We will be free to incoporate nonmedical visions of death's meanings, before and apart from our own encounter with terminal illnesses. To move more fully into prayerful relationship with God is to move into a new, more internalized relation to death and death imagery. This will deepen our inwardness and allow us to hear and speak with the voice of our souls. The appropriation of spiritual death language can open us to transcendence, so that we will be less like Ivan Ilych in our lives as well as our deaths. When we as Christians can grasp the power of the language of spiritual death, we will be able to go beyond "wild death" and its effects.

As Christians, we must seek to move further and further away from silence and denial. We have a stake in the death awareness movement's agenda. But this is not a once and for all journey, nor is it limited to certain public places and situations such as hospitals. The good news is that we know, as Christians, that we are accompanied in this travel. For us, it may become a parallel journey to those of Dante and Bunyan into the heart of death, sharing in Christ's death, and so into the heart of God.

Notes

Introduction

1. Arthur Kleinman, *The Illness Narratives* (New York: Basic Books, 1988) provides an eloquent statement of these points.
2. For a study of these works, see Lucy Bregman and Sara Thiermann, *First Person Mortal: Personal Narratives of Illness, Dying and Grief* (New York: Paragon House, 1995).
3. Philippe Ariès, *Western Attitudes toward Death: From the Middle Ages to the Present,* trans. Patricia M. Ranum (Baltimore: The Johns Hopkins University Press, 1974), 14.
4. Peter Van Ness, introduction to *Spirituality and the Secular Quest,* ed. Peter Van Ness, vol. 22 of the World Spirituality Series (New York: Crossroad, 1996), 5.
5. See, for example, Warren McWilliams, "Divine Suffering in Contemporary Theology," *Scottish Journal of Theology* 3 (1980): 35–53.
6. Stephen Crites, "Angels We Have Heard," in *Religion as Story,* ed. James Wiggin (New York: Harper and Row, 1975), 55.
7. Stephen Levine, *Who Dies?* (New York: Doubleday, 1982), 272.
8. Cathy Davidson, *36 Views of Mt. Fuji: On Finding Myself in Japan.* New York: Plume (Penguin Books, 1993), 228.

Chapter 1

1. Daniel Walker, *The Decline of Hell* (Chicago: University of Chicago Press, 1964), 4ff. See also Tony Walter, *The Eclipse of Eternity: A Sociology of the Afterlife* (Houndmills, England: Macmillan Press, 1996), 19.
2. Seward Hiltner, *Preface to Pastoral Theology* (New York: Abingdon Press, 1958), 83.
3. Peter Brown, *The Cult of the Saints* (Chicago: University of Chicago Press, 1981).
4. Joachim Jeremias, *Infant Baptism in the First Four Centuries* (Philadelphia: Westminster Press, 1960), 42.
5. Bede, *A History of the English Church and People,* trans. Leo Sherley-Price, rev. R. E. Latham (Harmondsworth, England: Penguin Books, 1968), 2.13. 127.
6. Jacques LeGoff, *The Birth of Purgatory,* trans. Arthur Goldhammer (Chicago: University of Chicago Press, 1984), 210ff.
7. *The Book of the Craft of Dying,* ed. Frances M. M. Comper (New York: Arno Press, 1977), 13.
8. Ibid., 28.
9. Ibid., 14. The author cites St. Bernard as the source of these words.

10. Steven Ozment, *The Reformation in the Cities* (New Haven: Yale University Press, 1980), 111.
11. John Bunyan, *The Pilgrim's Progress* (New York: New American Library, 1981), 148.
12. Ibid., 282.
13. Philippe Ariès, *The Hour of Our Death,* trans. Helen Weaver (New York: Vintage, 1982).
14. Ann Douglas, *The Feminization of American Culture* (New York: Avon Books, 1977).
15. Paul C. Rosenblatt, *Bitter, Bitter Tears* (Minneapolis: University of Minnesota Press, 1983).
16. Walter Rauschenbusch, *A Theology for the Social Gospel* (New York: Macmillan Co., 1918), 237.
17. Oscar Cullman, "Immortality of the Soul or Resurrection of the Dead?" in *Resurrection and Immortality,* ed. Krister Stendahl (New York: Macmillan Co., 1965), 17. Italics in original.
18. Ibid., 51.
19. Walter, *Eclipse of Eternity,* 191–95.

Chapter 2

1. Herman Feifel, ed., *The Meaning of Death* (New York: McGraw-Hill Book Co., 1959). See also Herman Feifel, ed., *New Meanings of Death* (New York: McGraw-Hill Book Co., 1977).
2. Margaretta K. Bowers et al., *Counseling the Dying* (San Francisco: Harper and Row, 1964). This was reissued in 1981.
3. Leo Tolstoy, *The Death of Ivan Ilych and Other Stories* (New York: New American Library, n.d.), 102.
4. Ibid., 131.
5. Ibid., 149.
6. Elisabeth Kübler-Ross, *On Death and Dying* (New York: Macmillan, 1969), 5.
7. Tolstoy, *Death of Ivan Ilych,* 135.
8. See chapter 8 of Philip Rieff, *Freud: The Mind of the Moralist* (Garden City, N.Y.: Doubleday, 1961). See also Peter Homans, *The Ability to Mourn: Disillusionment and the Social and Psychological Origin of Psychoanalysis* (Chicago: University of Chicago Press, 1989).
9. Sigmund Freud, *Totem and Taboo,* trans. James Strachey (London: Hogarth, 1957), 51.
10. Ernest Becker, *The Denial of Death* (New York: Free Press, 1973).
11. Robert J. Lifton, *The Broken Connection* (New York: Simon and Schuster, 1979), 49.
12. There are cautious and incautious presentations of these ideas. "Ecofeminism" rests on the above critique of Western masculine denigration of nature. Recent scholarly attention in religion, philosophy, and literature to the body in thought and culture rests upon the perspective summarized here. Whether or not what is female is *always* and inevitably linked to nature is an interesting and controversial question. One may certainly find systems of

thought that do not define nature in gender categories in exactly the same fashion that Western culture does.

13. Kübler-Ross, *On Death and Dying,* 13.

14. Samuel Southard, *Death and Dying: A Bibliographical Survey* (New York: Greenwood Press, 1991), xxx.

15. William F. May, *The Physician's Covenant: Images of the Healer in Medical Ethics* (Philadelphia: Westminster Press, 1983.)

16. Lael Wertenbaker, *The Death of a Man* (New York: Bantam Books, 1957), 120.

17. Elisabeth Kübler-Ross, ed., *Death: The Final Stage of Growth* (Englewood Cliffs, N.J.: Prentice-Hall, 1975).

18. Avery Weisman, *On Dying and Denying* (New York: Behavioral Publications, 1972), 213.

19. Abraham Maslow, *Toward a Psychology of Being,* 2d ed. (Princeton N.J.: D. Van Nostrand Co., 1968), 137.

20. See Paul Vitz, *Psychology as Religion: The Cult of Self-Worship* (Grand Rapids: Wm. B. Eerdmans, 1977).

21. Robert Bellah et al., *The Habits of the Heart: Individualism and Commitment in American Life* (Berkeley: University of California Press, 1985).

22. Bonnie Miller-McLemore, *Death, Sin and the Moral Life* (Atlanta: Scholars Press, 1988), 92–99.

23. Don Browning, *Religious Thought and the Modern Psychologies: A Critical Conversation in the Theology of Culture* (Philadelphia: Fortress Press, 1987), 75.

24. Wertenbaker, *Death of a Man,* 119.

Chapter 3

1. Lafcadio Hearn, *Gleanings in Buddha-Fields* (Boston: Houghton Mifflin Co., 1895), 86.

2. Clayton Naff, *About Face* (New York: Kodansha International, 1994), 256–57.

3. Richard C. Cabot and Russell L. Dicks, *The Art of Ministering to the Sick* (New York: Macmillan Co., 1957), 3. This work, first published in 1936, is a classic because it reveals the same problems and offers some of the same solutions decades in advance of the death awareness movement. Moreover, its treatment of many topics is more sensible and more balanced than much of what has been written recently.

4. Anne Simmonds, "Pastoral Perspectives in Intensive Care: Experiences of Doctors and Nurses with Dying Patients," *Journal of Pastoral Care* 53 (Fall 1997): 281.

5. Ibid., 280.

6. Charles Meyer, *Surviving Death: A Practical Guide to Caring for the Dying and Bereaved.* (Mystic, Conn.: Twenty-Third Publications, 1988), 9.

7. For an example of this trend, see Thomas Oden, *Pastoral Theology: Essentials of Ministry* (San Francisco: Harper and Row, 1983).

8. Victor Zorza and Rosemary Zorza, *A Way to Die* (New York: Alfred A. Knopf, 1980).

9. Paul Irion, *Hospice and Ministry* (Nashville: Abingdon Press, 1988), 20.

10. Dorothy C. H. Ley, "Spiritual Care in Hospice," in *Death and Spirituality,* ed. Kenneth Doka and John Morgan (Amityville, N.Y.: Baywood Publishing Co., 1993), 171.
11. Tolstoy, *Death of Ivan Ilych,* 143–44.

Chapter 4

1. Thomas Attig, *How We Grieve: Relearning the World* (New York: Oxford University Press, 1996).
2. Erich Lindemann, "Symptomatology and Management of Acute Grief," *American Journal of Psychiatry* 101 (1944): 141–48.
3. Kübler-Ross, *On Death and Dying,* 13.
4. Kenneth Keniston, *The Uncommitted: Alienated Youth in American Society* (New York: Dell Publishing Co., 1960).
5. Colin M. Parkes, *Bereavement: Studies of Grief in Adult Life* (New York: International Universities Press, 1972), 39–56.
6. William Worden, *Grief Counseling and Grief Therapy: A Handbook for the Mental Health Practitioner* (New York: Springer Publishing Co., 1982), 11–16.
7. Ibid., 16.
8. Attig, *How We Grieve,* 48.
9. Therese Rando, *Treatment of Complicated Mourning* (Champaign, Ill.: Research Press, 1993), 45.
10. See Rando's discussion of overlapping diagnoses and mourning's relation to posttraumatic stress disorder in *Treatment of Complicated Mourning,* 203, 570ff.
11. Rieff, *Freud,* 358 (see chap. 2, n. 8).
12. Kenneth Doka, ed., *Disenfranchised Grief: Recognizing Hidden Sorrow* (New York: Lexington Books, 1989).
13. Myra Blueblood-Langer, *In the Shadow of Illness* (Princeton N.J.: Princeton University Press, 1996).
14. See chapter 4 of Kübler-Ross, *On Death and Dying,* and Rando, *Treatment of Complicated Mourning,* 48ff.
15. Stewart Alsop, *Stay of Execution* (Philadelphia: J.B. Lippincott Co., 1973).
16. Kübler-Ross, *On Death and Dying,* 122–23.
17. *The Book of Common Prayer* (New York: Church Hymnal Corporation, 1979), 482–83.
18. Ibid., 481.
19. Ibid., 481.
20. Kenneth Mitchell and Herbert Anderson, *All Our Losses, All Our Griefs: Resources for Pastoral Care* (Philadelphia: Westminster Press, 1983), 142.
21. *The Book of Common Prayer,* 497.
22. Early examples of this are Audrey Gordon, "The Psychological Wisdom of the Law," in *Jewish Reflections on Death,* ed. Jack Riemer (New York: Schocken Books, 1974), 95–104; and Gary Gerson, "The Psychology of Grief and Mourning in Judaism," *Journal of Religion and Health* 16 (1977): 261–71.

Chapter 5

1. Lloyd Bailey, Sr., *Biblical Perspectives on Death* (Philadelphia: Fortress Press, 1979), 48–52.

2. Miller-McLemore, *Death, Sin and the Moral Life,* 124.

3. Ibid., 176.

4. Ibid., 134.

5. Albert Ritschl, *The Christian Doctrine of Justification and Reconciliation,* trans. H. R. Mackintosh and A. B. Macaulay (Clifton, N.J.: Reference Book Publishers, 1966), 95.

6. David Clark, *Death-Bed Scenes* (Philadelphia: Carlton and Phillips, 1855).

7. William V. Hocker, "Unsanctioned and Unrecognized Grief: A Funeral Director's Perspective," in Doka, *Disenfranchised Grief,* 257–58.

8. Norman Cousins, *Anatomy of an Illness* (New York: Bantam Books, 1979).

9. Albert Camus, *The Plague,* trans. Stuart Gilbert (New York: Alfred A. Knopf, 1948), 196ff.

10. Franz Kafka, *The Penal Colony* (New York: Schocken Books, 1961), 148–50.

Chapter 6

1. Elizabeth Stuart Phelps, *The Gates Ajar,* ed. Helen Sootin Smith (Cambridge, Mass.: Belknap Press, 1964), 92–97.

2. For a fuller discussion, see my *Death in the Midst of Life* (Grand Rapids: Baker Book House, 1992), 114ff.

3. Kübler-Ross, *On Death and Dying,* 15.

4. Weisman, *On Dying and Denying,* 213 (See chap. 2 n. 18).

5. JoAnn Kelley Smith, *Free Fall* (Valley Forge Pa.: Judson Press, 1975).

6. Ibid., 45.

7. David Watson, *Fear No Evil* (Wheaton, Ill.: Harold Shaw, 1984).

8. Terry Tempest Williams, *Refuge* (New York: Pantheon, 1991).

9. Davidson, *36 Views,* 227 (see intro., n. 8).

10. Ibid., 228.

11. See Jeanne DuPrau, *The Earth House* (Pound Ridge, N.Y.: New Chapter Press, 1992).

12. Rudolph Wurlitzer, *Hard Travel to Sacred Places* (Boston: Shambala, 1995).

13. Raymond Moody, *Life after Life* (New York: Bantam Books, 1975).

14. Lee Bailey and Jenny Yates, eds., *The Near-Death Experience: A Reader* (New York: Routledge & Kegan Paul, 1996), 3.

15. Allan Kellehear, *Experiences Near Death: Beyond Medicine and Religion* (New York: Oxford University Press, 1996), 132.

16. Carol Zaleski, *Otherworld Journeys* (New York: Oxford University Press, 1989).

17. Dannion Brinkley with Paul Perry, *Saved by the Light* (New York: Villard Books, 1994). Betty J. Eadie with Curtis Taylor, *Embraced by the Light* (New York: Bantam Books, 1994). Melvin Morse with Paul Perry, *Closer to the Light* (New York: Villard Books, 1990). Melvin Morse and Paul Perry, *Transformed by the Light* (New York: Ballantine Books, 1992). Kevin Randle, *To Touch the Light* (New York: Wondson Publications, 1994). Brad Steiger, *One with the Light* (New York: Signet, 1994).

18. Randle, *To Touch the Light,* 62.

19. Elisabeth Kübler-Ross, *On Children and Death* (New York: Macmillan Pub-

lishing Co., 1983), 141. In a public lecture, this image was further literalized as Kübler-Ross displayed a children's toy, a stuffed plush caterpillar that when turned inside out became a butterfly!

20. Maggie Callanan and Patricia Kelley, *Final Gifts* (New York: Poseidon Press, 1992), 102.
21. Ibid., 76.
22. Kübler-Ross, *On Death and Dying*, 113.
23. Callanan and Kelley, *Final Gifts*, 98.
24. Ibid., 110.
25. Ibid., 97.
26. David Royse, "The Near-Death Experience: Survey of Clergy's Attitudes and Knowledge," *Journal of Pastoral Care* 39 (1985):34.
27. Levine, *Who Dies?* 27 (see intro. n. 7).

INDEX

acceptance, 50, 52, 70, 74–76, 113, 116–17, 142
Acts, book of 7:55–56, 20
Acts of the Apostles, 20, 142, 180
Adam, 134, 137, 139, 141, 150
A.D.E.C. (Association for Death Education and Counseling), 44
afterlife, 20–25, 33–34, 155–76, 178
    See also Heaven; Hell; near death experience; Purgatory
AIDS, 115, 144–45, 146
AIDS Memorial Quilt (NAMES Project), 127–28
Alighieri, Dante. *See* Dante
Alsop, Stewart, 116
Anatomy of an Illness, 147
Anderson, Herbert, 121
angels, 10–11
anger, 26, 126, 149–50
Ariès, Philippe, 6, 20, 32, 51, 54, 119
Ars Moriendi, 25–28, 33, 40, 173
asceticism, 19, 29
Attig, Thomas, 108, 114
autobiographies, 6, 94, 160–64, 168

"bad deaths," 135, 141–142
baptism, 20
Bailey, Lee, 165–66
Bailey, Lloyd, 135
Becker, Ernest, 55

Bede, 21–22
"Being of Light," 165, 169, 174
    See also near death experience
Bellah, Robert, 69, 71
Bellamine, Robert, 25
bereavement. *See* mourning
Bible
    death in Old Testament, 134–35
    death in New Testament, 18, 38, 137–39
    reading, 84, 87
    See also death: Christian views of Jesus; passion narratives; Paul
"Big Secret," 166–67, 170, 172, 173, 176
birth, 60, 62–63
Black Death, 24
Blueblood-Langer, Myra, 115
The Book of the Craft of Dying.
    See Ars Moriendi
The Book of Common Prayer, 120–22
Burial Rite I, 119–21
Burial Rite II, 121–22
Brinkley, Dannion, 167
Brown, Peter, 19
Browning, Don, 71–73
Buddhism, 119, 163–64
    See also death: Buddhist views
Bultman, Rudolph, 178–80
Bunyan, John, 29–32, 155

See also death: Christian views; Jesus; passion narratives
therapy. See psychotherapy
Tillich, Paul, 7
Tolstoy, Leo, 48–50, 51, 56, 77
Torah, 123–24
transcendence, 93–95, 159, 188
Treatment of Complicated Mourning, 108–11

The Uncommitted, 104

Vietnam War, 61–62, 64, 103–104
Vietnam War Memorial, 104, 127
Vitz, Paul, 70
volunteers, 88, 92–93

Walter, Tony, 31, 38
war. See military imagery; Vietnam War; World War II
Watson, David, 160–61

A Way to Die, 88–89
Weber, Max, 29, 30
weeping, 39–40, 122
Weisman, Avery, 67, 158, 169
Wertenbaker, Lael, 64–65
widows, 106, 126
"wild death," 6, 12, 79, 80, 81, 94, 102, 176, 181, 183, 186, 188
Williams, Terry Tempest, 161–62
women, 32, 63, 130
See also feminization; gender imagery; nature; as feminine
Worden, William, 107–108
Wurlitzer, Rudoph, 164

Yates, Jenny, 165–66

Zaleski, Carol, 167
Zorza, Victor and Rosemary, 88–89